PISCES
21 FEBRUARY - 20 MARCH

PISCES

21 FEBRUARY - 20 MARCH

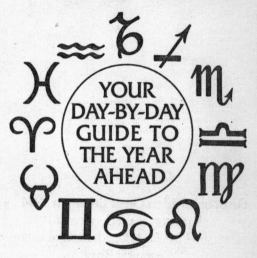

YOUR
DAY-BY-DAY
GUIDE TO
THE YEAR
AHEAD

‖ · PARRAGON · ‖

First published in Great Britain in 1994 by
Parragon Book Service Ltd
Unit 13-17 Avonbridge Industrial Estate
Atlantic Road
Avonmouth
Bristol BS11 9QD

Copyright © Parragon Book Service Ltd 1994

ISBN 1 85813 868 X

Printed and bound by Firmin-Didot (France),
Group Herissey. No d'impression : 28018.

CONTENTS

PISCES
21 FEBRUARY - 20 MARCH

THE FISH

The symbol of Pisces is two fishes, swimming in opposite directions but joined by a string linking their mouths. Why this sign should represent those born under the twelfth House of the Zodiac may not be immediately obvious, for the Piscean is anything but a cold fish! The clue lies in the fishes' environment – the water. Water is an element which air-breathing creatures like ourselves can only visit for short periods. This being so, the unworldly Piscean lives on a different level from the rest of humanity, swimming at ease through the deep waters of the spiritual world where others only paddle.

In ancient Babylon, the fishes represented the goddesses of the two great life-giving rivers, the Tigris and the Euphrates. The constellation was known as The Tails. The two fishes are often used to signify a pair of related but different forms of wisdom. One may represent human awareness, the other a more cosmic vision. They may also stand for the paired routes of learning and teaching.

Babylonian astronomers also knew this sign

as The Leash, referring to the string that unites the two fish. This leash may be a precious link that binds two halves into a perfect whole – but it may also signify bondage, inhibition and repression.

The story of the star sign comes from the Classical world. To escape the giant Typhon, Venus, goddess of love, and her son Cupid flung themselves into the River Euphrates and became fishes. The goddess Minerva placed the two fishes in the heavens to commemorate their escape.

THE PISCEAN CHARACTER

Pisces has been called 'the sign of the poet', for Pisceans have a window on a world others may rarely glimpse, and they spend most of their time looking out of it! Those born under the twelfth House of the Zodiac are dreamers of dreams, visionaries and fantasists. They're sensitive, imaginative, emotional and unworldly. They may well be psychically gifted, being more aware of the spiritual world than are most mortals.

With their heads in the clouds, Pisceans find it hard to see what's going on around their feet. Everyday matters may be a mystery to them. Practicality isn't a characteristic they're noted for, and even the most intelligent may find themselves at a loss when required to understand how, or even why, things work. They may come across to others as vague and woolly-minded when they're simply out of their element with the routines of day-to-day living.

Pisceans are better at dreaming than doing. They can be wonderfully creative at the planning stage of a new project, but often need someone else to put their plans into action. It's unkind to call them lazy: their brains and imaginations are working at full blast even if their hands are idling. However, it might be foolish to rely on them if a job needs doing. They rarely have a very strong grasp of priorities, or of time, and certainly aren't the most organized of people. Decision-making isn't their strong point either: they're too easily swayed by others.

It's hard to dislike a Piscean. They can be irritating when they're too far out of touch, but their essential sweetness and gentleness are endearing. They're sensitive to others' feelings, sometimes to the point where one suspects telepathy. They are easily aroused to sympathy, because they can imagine what it's like to be in another's shoes. If you're in trouble, you can rely on a Piscean to come and fish you out, even if it's at considerable cost to themselves. People matter to them, so they're willing to be generous with their time and their money. Pisces is sometimes called 'the sign of the healer' and these born humanitarians are eager to help and heal wherever they can.

In any case, it would be unfair to dislike a Piscean when they're all too ready to dislike themselves. The Piscean ego is a sadly fragile thing. Hypersensitive to the point of neurosis, they can be shattered by mild criticism. They're vulnerable creatures who just aren't assertive enough to cope with the rough and tumble of ordinary social encounters. Other people can drive them to anxiety attacks or unpredictable mood swings. They need constant emotional reassurance to stay on an even keel. Be cruel to a Piscean, and they'll swim away and hide in the weeds away from human contact.

Vulnerable they may be, but stick-in-the-mud they certainly aren't. People can hurt them, but they're always open to new encounters. Sensitivity can be their weak spot, but can also be a strength which enables them to adapt to new situations. They're attracted to the unknown, and often positively adventurous. They're eager to try new foods, visit new places, experiment with new pleasures and offer a welcome to new friends. Pisces can get a lot out of life – though often they need to assert their right to do so a bit more forcibly.

PISCES AT WORK

Even dreamers have to work, and so long as Pisceans find the right niche they have a real contribution to make on the work front. They're bubbling with ideas, not afraid to experiment, and a constant source of inspiration, innovation and encouragement to others. Finding the right kind of work is perhaps more crucial to this sign than to any other.

Repetitive, undemanding work may suit Pisceans who don't hanker after the fast lane, simply because it leaves their minds free to wander.

Pisceans with a bit more vim are likely in such a situation to let their minds wander too far from the job and make ridiculous mistakes. Tasks which demand an unwavering eye to tiny details are unlikely to suit any Piscean. They have quick brains, and a gift for knowledge – acquiring it, using it, and passing it on. Some may be tempted to become perpetual students. Others have considerable success in the teaching profession, where they can combine educational skills with pastoral care. Their gifts for understanding others and caring about them make them wonderful teachers, whether they're cuddling a scared primary school entrant or having a drink with a group of undergraduates.

Few Pisceans fancy being the boss in any working establishment. It ties them down too much! As employers, they have one great virtue: they genuinely care about the welfare of their staff. Also, they have one great vice: procrastination. They've very little sense of time, or of urgency, are weak at prioritizing, and can defer decisions till the cows come home.

Another Piscean quality may count as virtue, vice, or both at once. It's that fertility of imagination, constantly popping out bright ideas to improve productivity, work conditions or anything else in sight. Some of these ideas are marvellous. Some are duds! The Piscean boss doesn't always discriminate between the two, and in any case may drive employees mad with this passion for change and innovation. With Pisces in charge, there's always a risk the work force will end up confused and unco-operative.

Most Pisceans make better employees than employers. They're still full of ideas, but it helps to have someone in charge to vet these before any are put into action. Mind you, the character and intelligence of that person in charge matters enormously. Pisceans won't work well under anyone they can't respect, or whom they feel is not supportive. If they're happy in their position, they're a valuable asset to any employer. They're popular with workmates, and can help to forge a batch of individuals into a cohesive team.

Creative work is almost a must for Pisceans. Their imagination and sensitivity cry out for expression, and they are often successful as writers, artists or designers. Their needs can also be answered by work centred on the spiritual world. They may choose to enter the established church or head for an alternative lifestyle as druids, mediums or even white witches. If they choose to work in a practical line, it's likely to be humanitarian idealism that directs them. Many Pisceans make a beeline for the caring professions, where they can pour their energies out for the benefit of others. They may become social workers or prison visitors, or work in a hospice. Those whom the planets have blessed with more practical skills than the typical Piscean may become dedicated doctors. Some Pisceans find it easier to care for animals than people, and may seek work in this line. They'll be drawn to the underdog rather than the pampered lapdog, and are more likely to work in an animal shelter than a poodle parlour.

PISCES AT PLAY

Many of Pisces' favourite leisure hour pursuits are solitary ones. The Piscean imagination is company enough! In fact, most Pisceans actually need time on their own to give their imagination a completely free hand.

Every Piscean needs to express their creative side. Many are artistically gifted, so painting or sketching may be their delight. Often they excel at landscape painting, and may spend long quiet hours alone with their easel and their inspiration. Others prefer to express themselves in writing. Beautifully crafted short stories or poems are more typical than long, rambling novels. They will take equal pleasure in reading. Craftwork is generally less popular, though Pisceans of both sexes may find embroidery or tapestry a relaxing employment. They are also often attracted to studying a specialist area – ferns, church architecture, local history – and may become unobtrusively expert in their chosen field.

Outdoor pursuits also offer opportunities for peace and quiet. Long country walks – more ambles than rambles – may appeal, with other solitary pursuits such as fishing or bird-watching. Pisces likes to potter in the garden. Bringing a whole garden under control often seems a bit brutal to this gentle soul, and the Piscean gardener is happiest tending specimen plants in the greenhouse. The joy of joys might be a specialist alpine house where each pot or trough is a perfect miniature landscape. Outside the glasshouse, tell-tale signs of a Piscean gardener include bird-baths, bird-tables, bat-boxes and a pond occupied by frogs and newts. Shrubs and flowers will include a high proportion of species chosen to attract butterflies, and there's likely to be a secluded corner where nettles are left undisturbed to feed the caterpillars.

Pisceans often get a lot of pleasure from pets, and the pleasure isn't one-sided, for they're caring and considerate owners. They may err on the sentimental side towards their animals, and end up with an order from the vet to put Puss on a diet or Fido on a leash. However, they won't commit the unintentional cruelties of less imaginative types. The Piscean's dog isn't going to live on a chain attached to a damp kennel; their cat won't be expected to catch its own food; and even their hamster isn't going to live a bleak life in a little plastic prison cell.

Don't get the idea that Pisces has no time for other people when it comes to playtime. So long as the Piscean can choose times to be alone, they'll also choose times to seek out company and enjoy a lively social life. They don't like to be tied to a regular timetable, so they're not great club-joiners. They lack a competitive streak, so they're not great games-players either. They're entertaining conversationalists, good listeners and generally welcome wherever they go.

Pisces is also adventure-loving. Rough contact sports like rugby are unlikely to appeal, but the challenge of scuba diving, mountaineering, and such exploratory hobbies is irresistible. Travel to out-of-the-way places is another favourite. Lying among a row of sunbathers on a beach, or enjoying the facilities of a holiday camp isn't the Piscean idea of a holiday. They're more likely to fancy llama-trekking in the Peruvian mountains, whale-watching off Greenland or diving for submerged wrecks off the Orkneys.

PISCES AT HOME

Home for Pisceans is a place of refuge, and others may be struck first by the peaceful, soothing atmosphere. Piscean decor is more timeless than trendy, although many Pisceans have a weakness for the swirling lines of Art Nouveau. Strident hues are out, as are furnishings designed to catch the eye. Look for muted colours and unobtrusive good taste. This is certainly not the same as being dull or characterless. Pisces has a collector's eye, though not the full-blown collecting habit, and will have picked up a number of items which would stand out if they didn't harmonize so well with the room. Many Pisceans will have a room set apart for their own use, whether they call it a study, den, workshop or sewing room.

Family life brings out the best in Pisceans.

They're loving and sensitive parents who find a creative pleasure in satisfying their children's wants and needs. They won't ignore childish moods or brush off childish worries, and are generous with their time and attention. They may err on the side of spoiling their children, denying their own needs in order to satisfy childish wants. As disciplinarians they're often non-starters, for they hate to say 'No' and prefer to appeal to a child's better nature. With some children this approach works, but tougher, more self-centred kids may take advantage of soppy old Pisceans and walk all over them.

Piscean parents give their children a head start in the arts side of their education. They'll provide a background rich in art, literature and music, and will be eager to encourage creative interests, such as painting, dancing and playing an instrument. They'll also be demonstrative parents who encourage their offspring to express their emotions freely. Their children are unlikely to grow up emotionally repressed; it's more likely they'll be too much the other way.

The Piscean mother may be a bit of a worry-guts. She'll fret about everything from teeth-cleaning to vitamin intake, and may become over-protective outside the home. A Piscean Dad will be much more involved with his offspring than many other fathers. He's a real New Man when it comes to nappy-changing or attending to scratched knees, though it never occurs to him that he's doing anything some fathers wouldn't. He won't try to force his children in directions they don't want to go, but he's always ready to introduce them to new ideas and to encourage their budding interests.

The Piscean child needs a highly supportive background in order to blossom. Without emotional security and parental encouragement they may be shy, nervous and withdrawn. They're gentle creatures, with a natural kindness and generosity rare among the very young. They may be slow to explore the outside world. They're often happiest in their own company drawing or making up stories, and need to be encouraged – not pushed – to go out and make friends. The sports field is unlikely to attract them as much as the library. A wise parent will consider dancing lessons, skating or even karate classes to make physical exercise more attractive to them. Daydreaming may be a problem at school, where they need a teacher who can capture their imagination. It's all too easy for the little Piscean to under-perform in class, preferring to switch off and think of something more interesting!

Pets are likely to be very much part of the Piscean family scene, and will be treated as members of the family. Piscean adults can find a lot of emotional security in a pet's affection, and the Piscean child in particular will benefit from having an animal of their own to care for.

PISCES AND MONEY

Pisces and no money is more often the case! Cash slips through Piscean hands like water: after all, it's there to be spent. The typical Piscean is the bank manager's nightmare. Send them a letter about their overdraft and they'll be surprised, even mildly hurt. They had no idea they'd spent so much, and will put off that depressing visit to the bank to sort things out in the hope that some more money may turn up in time to solve the problem. In fact, they'll probably go on a shopping spree to comfort themselves!

Savings schemes have little appeal to Pisces, though they'll be willing to pay out for Premium Bonds or the Pools: the exciting chance of a big win is more appealing than the certainty of a boring old planned investment. They're suckers for raffle tickets, draws, tombolas, anything where the element of chance applies.

Spending on luxuries is a Piscean weakness. You won't find Pisces hunting through the supermarket for special offers and cut-price brands: nothing but the best will do. If money's tight, well, fish don't have horns to draw in! That adventurous imagination can get the Piscean into financial deep waters as well. They'll spurn a house that matches their practical needs and income, in favour of the marvellous potential of a tumbledown mansion that needs a fortune spent on it. On the other hand, the spiritual side of Pisces means their idea of luxury may be freedom from worldly goods. Some will be just as happy living in a commune with like-minded souls, where boring old money needn't be part of their life at all.

Pisces is as ready to give money away as to spend it. The Piscean is generous to friends, family and even casual acquaintances. They're responsive to charity appeals and vulnerable to hard-luck stories. No, the bank manager just doesn't stand a chance!

PISCES AND HEALTH

From ancient times, astrologers have linked each sign of the Zodiac with a specific part of the body. The sign of Pisces was calculated to rule the feet, and in consequence Pisceans tend to be more prone than most to weaknesses in this area. They should take care of their feet, especially when choosing shoes. Ill-fitting shoes won't stop at deforming Piscean feet with corns and bunions, but will enforce bad posture with the risk of significant damage to the spine. Pisceans also tend to be highly vulnerable to colds and influenza, and need to live a healthy life in order to fight these off.

Pisces can be the bane of the doctor's life, because this sign often responds oddly to prescribed drugs. Antibiotics in particular may have an adverse effect. Of course, there's also the problem that few Pisceans will remember to take their medicine regularly. They are all too likely to forget to take a pill for several days and then swallow a handful at once to catch up.

Generally speaking, Pisceans tend to be better at looking after others than themselves. They find it all too easy to neglect sensible rules of diet, and are not particularly attracted to exercise. They are very likely to be overweight or underweight. The really healthy Piscean is usually one who has a caring partner to look after that side of their life! Without the emotional support they need, they may turn to comfort eating or to the bottle. Alcohol can be a real danger to Pisces, and the Piscean who drinks like a fish is in trouble!

PISCES AND THE OPPOSITE SEX

The dreamer can be a disappointing lover, for Pisceans are often too romantic for their own good. They're looking for the girl whose foot fits the glass slipper, or for the enchanted frog who awaits their kiss, and a partner of flesh and blood is unlikely to live up to their dreams.

Pisces wants emotional support, but that may not be the same thing as security. Ideally, they'd like to have a source of ready sympathy and support on tap, and to swim back to it at times of their own choosing. Offer them a permanent commitment, and they're quick to spot the fish-hook in the middle of the bait. The romantic Piscean falls in love easily, but the minute they feel themselves being reeled in they start fighting the line. They need freedom within a relationship, and may demand too much of it to be acceptable to many partners. A long-term relationship only stands a chance if the lover is also a friend.

Because a real-life partnership can never offer as much as the imagined one round the corner, infidelity is a natural Piscean weakness. Pisces has an incurably roving eye, and can resist anything except temptation! They do hate hurting people, though, and can make a terrible mess of the end of an affair in their attempts to avoid an emotional scene.

This doesn't mean Pisces can't make a go of a partnership. Once they make a commitment to marriage, they may remain faithful out of that natural idealism, and once they've started a family, they're unwilling to let children down.

PARTNERSHIPS

Pisces and Aries

Opposites attract, but whether they stay attracted is another matter. The unworldly Piscean and worldly-wise Arian may expand each other's horizons – or they may just infuriate each other! Give it a whirl: if it isn't going to work out, you'll soon know! This relationship has got to be one of equal rights for both partners to stand any chance of success.

Pisces and Taurus

Sorry, but this is asking for trouble! This relationship is only likely to get off the ground if Taurus has had a bump and Pisces comes to kiss it better. It's a match founded on a misunderstanding. Once the bull's feeling better, what on earth is the feeling fish going to do? They've nothing in common, and little to say to each other. The sooner Pisces swims off, the better for both parties.

Pisces and Gemini

Life won't be easy for this combination, or for their associates. Team up Gemini's frailty of purpose with Piscean daydreams, and who's going to sort out the practicalities of life? This couple will need a nursemaid if they're going to survive! Mind you, they'll never be short of friends who are usually willing to come to the rescue, and dine out on the funny story.

Pisces and Cancer

These two make a promising pair. Shared dreams may provide a surprisingly solid foundation for a relationship. Both sides are good at seeing the other's point of view, and can be happy in the same environment. Pisces can see past that tough Cancerian shell and knows the crab isn't crabby at all. Also, Cancer can appreciate the Piscean's need for an occasional dose of privacy without feeling spurned.

Pisces and Leo

Pisces may be attracted to Leo, but the lion's likely to have other fish to fry! This tends to be a very one-sided (and short-lived) relationship. A shared creative interest may draw these two together for a while, but there's no sexual spark there and very little chance of real liking. Differences in lifestyle and lack of mutual respect soon have them drifting apart.

Pisces and Virgo

They don't really have a language in common – but it's surprising how far they can get with smiles and signs! Logical, reasonable Virgo and intuitive, unreasonable Pisces may be different enough to avoid the head-on clash you might expect. It's a relationship of equals, each prepared to give the other space. It may be less sexually exciting than some combinations, but strong on affection.

Pisces and Libra
What an unlikely mixture! It's so unlikely it might even work. These two have so little in common it's surprising they ever met. If matters go any further, there has to be something special going for them, and there is! When Libra and Pisces fall for each other – and that's rare – it's a magic moment, and a fairytale come true. Libra can make Piscean daydreams come true for both of them.

Pisces and Scorpio
The scorpion scores high on the list of suitable partners for the fussy fish. Scorpio can be difficult, but this brings out the most understanding side of Pisces. Pisces is less likely to stray in this relationship, for it continues to present a challenge rather than settling into dull domesticity. An uninhibited and affectionate sex life satisfies the physical and emotional needs of both parties.

Pisces and Sagittarius
Disappointing! The archer's way off target this time, while Pisces is likely to be a fish out of water in this partnership. They have such different expectations of each other, and of what relationships should be in general. They may set off in a spirit of optimism, but end up with their high hopes dashed and promises broken. Chances are slightly better, though, if Pisces is on the cusp with Aries.

Pisces and Capricorn
This is a real gamble. Whether it comes off depends
on such subtle shadings of character that it's all
down to the individuals concerned. A near-miss is
the most likely result, and in matters of the heart a
miss is definitely as good as a mile. However, when
the Pisces-Capricorn combination does work, it's a
sure-fire winner and a partnership for life. Are you
feeling lucky?

Pisces and Aquarius
There won't be much equality between these two,
but so long as one is content to live in the other's
shadow, they may be much happier together than
outsiders expect. It's a good match for those who
enjoy role playing. Secretly, the dominant partner
admits to a surprising degree of dependence on the
other, while their mate's apparent submission may
be all on the surface.

Pisces and Pisces
Too many fish may spoil the broth! A strong sexual
chemistry and the imagination to lift the whole
affair into a realm of fantasy give this relationship a
lively start, but two Pisceans won't keep the impetus
going for long. At the first disagreement, they may
use their understanding of each other to nip just
where it hurts. It won't be long before they swim off
in opposite directions.

PISCEAN EMBLEMS

Your number: 7. This number symbolizes knowledge
and spiritual awareness. From ancient times it has
been regarded as a mystical and magical digit which
bridges the gulf between mortal and immortal
wisdom. In ancient Babylon, this number was sacred
to the deity Ishtar, who was at once goddess of love
and 'the lady of battles', ruling both fertility and
destruction. The mystic number is well suited to
Pisces, most mystical of signs.

Your day: Thursday. Sometimes known as
Thunderday, in classical times this day was
dedicated to thunder god Jove. The name Thursday
comes from Thor, Norse god of thunder. Many of
the Norse gods were highly mystical, but Thor, 'Old
Redbeard', was always the one with the common
touch, the most accessible of divinities. On the one
hand this suggests Pisces' ease of access to the
spiritual plane, but it may also be a reminder to be
content with the lower reaches of the mystical
world, and not despise the mundane.

Your birthstone: moonstone. This silvery variety of
feldspar takes its name from its moonlight colour.
Inevitably, it has strong lunar associations and is
linked with the mystical world, fertility, and the
feminine. Alternative birthstones for Pisces are
aquamarine or blue lace agate.

Your material: bronze. Bronze is a mixed metal,
created by combining copper and tin. The reference

is to Pisces' mixed nature, which combines the spiritual with the worldly. It is also a reminder that the mixture is stronger than either element alone. Other materials associated with this sign are tin, coral and satin.

Your colour: violet. Traditionally this is a mystical colour, for it is created by the union of two primary colours, red and blue. Its associations are with meditation and consciousness-raising, both very close to the Piscean heart. However, it also denotes sorrow, mourning and penitence. Easily-wounded Pisces should be warned against giving grief too warm a welcome, and letting sorrow degenerate into self-pity.

Your flower: white foxglove. Tradition associates the foxglove with the fairy world. The name is said to be a corruption of 'folk's glove', referring to 'the fair folk', as fairies were once termed. It was supposed to be impossible to cultivate the white foxglove, which would only grow, according to legend, when planted by the fairies themselves. It's an apt choice for unworldly Pisces.

Your tree: willow. In classical times, the willow was sacred to the moon goddess and has long had strong associations with witches. Traditionally, its influence is largely benign. It was known as 'witches' aspirin' since the leaves and bark were used as an effective folk remedy to cure the pains of rheumatism. That alone makes it an appropriate emblem for Pisces, the sign of the healer. However, the willow has an equally ancient association with sorrow, in particular that of lost love. Like the colour violet, it's another reference to Piscean vulnerability.

The Cusp-Born Piscean

Are you sure you are a Piscean? If you were born at the beginning of Pisces, that is on the cusp between Pisces and Aquarius, you may find you are more of an Aquarian than a Piscean. If you were born at the end of Pisces, on the cusp with Aries, you may be more of an Arian. Given your exact time and place of birth, a professional astrologer can calculate which sign presided over your birth: you may even not be an Piscean at all! Even if you are definitely ruled by Pisces, the cusp-born Piscean will often be strongly influenced by the neighbouring sign. In such cases, you may find it helpful to consult the horoscope for Aquarius or Aries, as the case may be.

For those born in the first few days of Pisces, the influence of Aquarius can exaggerate the natural Piscean character. Pisceans born on the cusp with Aquarius are even more volatile than usual. They flicker about like minnows in the stream, darting from one mood to another. It's practically impossible to pin them down in the real world. Ideals may matter more to them than flesh-and-blood people, and they spend their time chasing rainbows.

In contrast, for those born in the last days of Pisces, the influence of Aries adds a dash of assertiveness. Pisceans born on the cusp with Aries tend to be tougher and more purposeful than the unmixed Piscean, though much subtler about it than the true Arian. The combination is a happy one, for they can dream great dreams and are able to put them into action.

FAMOUS PISCEANS

Sidney Poitier, American film actor (20 February, 1927)

Dame Marie Rambert, British ballet eminence (20 February, 1888)

Honoré Daumier, French painter and draughtsman (20 February, 1808)

Jilly Cooper, British author and journalist (21 February, 1937)

Nina Simone, American jazz singer and pianist (21 February, 1934)

Hubert de Givenchy, French fashion designer (21 February, 1927)

W.H. Auden, Anglo-American poet (21 February, 1907)

Julie Walters, British film and TV actress (22 February, 1950)

Robert Baden-Powell, British Boy Scout founder (22 February, 1857)

George Washington, 1st President of the United States (22 February, 1732)

Peter Fonda, American film actor (23 February, 1940)

George Frederick Handel, German-British composer (23 February, 1685)

Samuel Pepys, British diarist (23 February, 1633)

Alain Prost, French motor-racing ace (24 February, 1955)

Dennis Waterman, British TV actor (24 February, 1948)

George Harrison, British musician; ex-Beatle (25 February, 1943)

Enrico Caruso, Italian operatic tenor (25 February, 1873)

Pierre Renoir, French Impressionist painter (25 February, 1841)

Johnny Cash, American country and western star (26 February, 1932)

Fats Domino, American rock 'n' roll singer and pianist (26 February, 1928)

W.F. Cody ('Buffalo Bill'), American showman (26 February, 1846)

Victor Hugo, French writer (26 February, 1802)

Paddy Ashdown, British Liberal Democrat leader (27 February, 1941)

Elizabeth Taylor, Anglo-American film actress (27 February, 1932)

John Steinbeck, American novelist (27 February, 1902)

Vincente Minelli, American film director (28 February, 1913)

Charles Blondin, French tight-rope walker (28 February, 1824)

Jimmy Dorsey, American big-band leader (29 February, 1904)

John Holland, Irish-American submarine inventor (29 February, 1840)

Gioacchino Rossini, Italian operatic composer (29 February, 1792)

Roger Daltrey, British rock star and actor (1 March, 1945)

David Niven, British film actor and writer (1 March, 1910)

Glenn Miller, American big-band leader (1 March, 1904)

Frederic Chopin, Polish composer and pianist (1 March, 1810)

Ian Woosnam, British golf champion (2 March, 1958)

Dame Naomi James, New Zealand yachtswoman (2 March, 1949)

Mikhail Gorbachev, Russian statesman (2 March, 1931)

Kurt Weill, German-American composer (2 March, 1900)

Fatima Whitbread, British Olympic athlete (3 March, 1961)

Miranda Richardson, British TV and film actress (3 March, 1958)

Jean Harlow, American film actress (3 March, 1911)

Patrick Moore, British astronomer and TV presenter (4 March, 1923)

Antonio Vivaldi, Italian composer (4 March, 1678)

Elaine Paige, British musical star (5 March, 1952)

Rex Harrison, British stage and film actor (5 March, 1905)

Hector Villa-Lobos, Brazilian composer (5 March, 1887)

Dame Kiri Te Kanawa, New Zealand operatic soprano (6 March, 1944)

Valentina Tereshkova, Russian astronaut (6 March, 1937)

Elizabeth Barrett Browning, British poet (6 March, 1806)

Lou Reed, American rock singer (2 March, 1944)

Cyrano de Bergerac, French writer and duelist (6 March, 1619)

Michelangelo, Italian painter, sculptor and poet (6 March, 1475)

Rik Mayall, British TV and film comedian (7 March, 1958)

Ivan Lendl, Czechoslovakian tennis champion (7 March, 1960)

Maurice Ravel, French composer (7 March, 1875)

Edwin Landseer, British animal painter and sculptor (7 March, 1802)

David Wilkie, British Olympic swimmer (8 March, 1955)

Lynn Seymour, Canadian ballerina (8 March, 1939)

Cyd Charisse, American dancer and film actress (8 March, 1921)

Kenneth Grahame, British author (8 March, 1859)

Bobby Fischer, American chess master (9 March, 1943)

Yuri Gagarin, Soviet astronaut; first in space (9 March, 1934)

André Courrèges, French fashion designer (9 March, 1913)

HRH The Prince Edward, youngest son of Queen Elizabeth II (10 March, 1964)

Bix Beiderbecke, American jazz musician (10 March, 1903)

Rupert Murdoch, Australian-American media mogul (11 March, 1931)

Douglas Adams, British author (11 March, 1952)

Dorothy Gish, American silent screen star (11 March, 1898)

Sir Malcolm Campbell, British speed-record breaker (11 March, 1885)

Liza Minelli, American singer and film actress (12 March, 1946)

Vaslav Nijinsky, Russian ballet dancer (12 March, 1890)

Neil Sedaka, American singer and songwriter (13 March, 1950)

Daniel Lambert, British famous fat man (728lb/330kg) (13 March, 1770)

Tessa Sanderson, British Olympic athlete (14 March, 1957)

Michael Caine, British film actor (14 March, 1933)

Albert Einstein, German-Swiss scientist (14 March, 1879)

Terence Trent d'Arby, American popular singer (15 March, 1961)

General Andrew Jackson, President of the United States (15 March, 1767)

Bernardo Bertolucci, Italian film director (16 March, 1940)

Jerry Lewis, American stage and film comedian (16 March, 1926)

Leo McKern, British film and TV actor (16 March, 1920)

Rudolf Nureyev, Russian ballet star and director (17 March, 1938)

Nat 'King' Cole, American singer and pianist (17 March, 1917)

Kate Greenaway, British artist and illustrator (17 March, 1846)

Pat Eddery, British champion jockey (18 March, 1952)

John Updike, American novelist (18 March, 1932)

Robert Donat, British stage and film actor (18 March, 1905)

Wilfred Owen, British poet of World War I (18 March, 1893)

Nikolai Rimsky-Korsakov, Russian composer (18 March, 1844)

Glenn Close, American film actress (19 March, 1947)

Ursula Andress, Swiss film actress (19 March, 1936)

Sergei Diaghilev, Russian ballet impresario (19 March, 1872)

Wyatt Earp, American lawman of the 'Old West' (19 March, 1848)

Dr. David Livingstone, British missionary-explorer (19 March, 1813)

Dame Vera Lynn, British popular singer (20 March, 1917)

Beniamino Gigli, Italian operatic tenor (20 March, 1890)

Henrik Ibsen, Norwegian playwright (20 March, 1823)

NOVEMBER 1994

WORK

Your fertile imagination will enable you to solve knotty problems and scramble over obstacles in your path. You may refuse to recognize your own limitations, but this is no bad thing, for in fact you can get further than boring old common sense suggests. The thoughts and actions of colleagues will be easy to read. You can work out which way they're going to jump, and keep one step ahead without too much difficulty. Pisceans who are tired of being a big fish in a small pond have their chance to swim upstream towards the main lake. If you take this opportunity, watch out en route for tempting bait which conceals a hook! Before embarking on any project, be sure your enthusiasm is directed towards a worthy goal, or you may fritter away your energies pointlessly. Don't be too ready to trust a colleague who claims to be on your side, but encourages you to neglect an important responsibility.

HOME

Home life is happy and productive, and you can think about long-term plans. If the only thing you've put away for a rainy day is your umbrella, it's time to start a sensible savings scheme. Building, decorating and repair work are well aspected. Your social life could take a bit of a back seat to domestic interests, but you'll be able to pick it up again easily enough when you're ready. Part-time or evening

which you'll be uncomfortable later. The right kind of exercise will help to dissipate some of your energy and leave you feeling calmer. Try dance, aerobics, yoga exercises or circuit training. Your mind will benefit from similar treatment: set it a creative challenge to work on. Luckily, loved ones are supportive and time spent among them will help you to feel more in tune with what's going on around you. Pisceans who are engaged in study plans will find themselves able to tackle difficult concepts with ease, but need to make an effort where background reading is concerned.

ROMANCE

Idealizing the object of your romantic interest will lead to disappointment. Get back into the real world! Admittedly there's a shortage of Prince Charmings and fairy princesses, but there's a very nice frog out there who's willing to return your kisses and croak some very sweet somethings into your ear. Partnerships which are stuck in a rut shouldn't be left there. Use all that spare energy of yours to get them back on the road and heading for the bright lights. This month love is something of a chameleon, ready to take its colour from its surroundings. Dull routine and dreary places will make your love life look boring, but romance will blossom in new haunts, so get ready to explore.

OCTOBER 1994

WORK
You've plenty of potential this month and every chance of achieving your goals. You're on an energy high which enables you to make quick decisions and zoom through your work at top speed. However, your physical strength may not be up to your mental energy. Slow down a bit to avoid ending the month in a state of exhaustion. You may be short on patience with other people's dilly-dallying, intolerant of caution and rather too keen to have your own way. You can get away with wilfully ignoring instructions some of the time, but if you do it once too often you'll have to eat humble pie in the face of an official reprimand. There's a lot going for you: cultivate some common sense if you want to make the most of it. Interviews need handling with care. Your positive mood may come across, quite inaccurately, as brashness and bumptiousness, and your real virtues may not be apparent to anyone who does not know you well.

HOME
Nervous tension is likely to create some discomfort on the home front. Be aware of the fact that you're uncharacteristically fidgety, intolerant and argumentative, and try to slow down enough to listen to others. Any plans for redecorating or refurbishing might be better left until you've got your balance back, or you may create an effect with

classes, especially if there is a strong academic content, will answer your social needs as well as stimulating your mind. Relationships with youngsters, whether they're your own or someone else's, will be rewarding. You are invited to get involved with a scheme to help disabled children. You can make a very positive contribution in terms of new ideas, so don't let shyness hold you back.

ROMANCE

Instinct tells you to run away from a stormy emotional scene. You'll do better to stand and fight, or at least face up to issues which need tackling now. Change is in the air. For partnerships with a strong foundation, this is a time of growth and exploration. Where the foundations are weak, cracks appear in the walls and you'll have to decide which direction you want to take. If there are strengths worth salvaging in the relationship, go back to basics and rebuild from the bottom up. However, some Pisceans may have to face up to the fact that they have been building on sand, and accept that it's time to make a new start elsewhere. A new romance will go swimmingly for Fish who have been floating solo for a while. Music is the food of love this month: you may meet someone special at a concert, or come to an understanding while listening to a favourite tape.

DECEMBER 1994

WORK

Tasks can be completed successfully and will bring satisfactory recognition, but you will have to rethink plans made earlier. Flexibility is all-important this month. Be prepared to sacrifice a short-term ambition to bring yourself closer to a much more significant goal. The help of a dull but dependable colleague will be invaluable to a major project: if you pick a more exciting high flyer to work with you on this, they'll provide brighter conversation but far less practical input. Workplace gossip is worth listening to, but add a good pinch of salt. Late in the month, you get wind of welcome new responsibilities, possibly entailing a complete job change. Pisceans employed in the caring professions are likely to be working long hours and finding the rewards fewer and further between than usual. Put your back into unpromising tasks. Things will pick up by mid-month when your endeavours bear fruit.

HOME

Domestic affairs are a maze through which you have to pick your way to find the right exit. You are faced with many choices of direction, and it will be all too easy to hover about in the mists of indecision. Be resolute, and listen to what loved ones have to say: they will prove more reliable guides through this tangle than you imagine. A lively social life offers a respite from difficulties at home. Enjoy it, but don't be tempted to neglect your domestic responsibilities. When a child confides a secret, you'll have a tricky time balancing out the need to take action while respecting their confidence. It can be done though, and your efforts will ensure that you keep the youngster's trust. A back problem won't go away until you replace an item of furniture which is causing it. Change your favourite chair or buy a new mattress or even a whole new bed.

ROMANCE

Communication will be constructive, whether you're talking to a partner of many years' standing or a new romantic interest who has just entered the scene. It's important to express your feelings as well as to discuss joint plans. Pillow talk with a partner, though apparently casual, will open your eyes to a weakness in your situation which you can do something about. Jealousy will be destructive. If it creeps into your relationship, draw it out into the open and talk things over in order to prevent grievous misunderstandings. Avoid casual liaisons this month or you'll find yourself in deeper water than you anticipated. An affair with a colleague is likely to be ill-starred from the start, especially if you have to keep things under wraps for fear of discovery.

JANUARY

1. SUNDAY

Happy New Year! You'll make a late start to the day (assuming you got to bed at all last night!) and you won't feel like doing anything strenuous. One domestic job will demand urgent attention, however; don't push it off on to a partner. Make resolutions to dream less and do more in 1995, and to be less sensitive to what people think of you. You know you've got it in you to succeed; now make others believe it.

2. MONDAY

Mind your manners if you're spending a holiday with relatives or friends. They have their own ways of doing things, and a good guest will conform to them. The health of a child may give some cause for concern, but it's only a passing upset. Home or away, you'll be part of a large gathering tonight. Young Pisceans who want to stand out like a shark in a bowl of goldfish should wear their lucky colour.

3. TUESDAY

Some time today you are likely to visit a relative or friend in hospital. Continue your mission of cheering people up with a telephone call to a long-neglected friend living far away. If you're back at work, it will take you some time to get started, but by mid-afternoon it'll be all systems go. You may have to work overtime because others are absent. You'll find no holds are barred in an all-in amorous encounter tonight.

4. WEDNESDAY

Important events will take place behind closed doors today. You'll be shut out, but a friend may help you put an ear to the keyhole. Keep silent for the time being about anything you hear: rumour-mongering could do you considerable harm. Curb a sudden urge to live dangerously in the romantic sphere. If you give a come-on sign tonight, the traffic will get much heavier than you expected, and you may be run down.

5. THURSDAY

Routine tasks at work or in the home will take up most of your day. You will be boosted when a loved one praises you for what seems to you a trivial accomplishment. A shopping trip will be made difficult by travel hitches, and you will not get everything you need. A takeaway meal, or dinner in a local restaurant if you have any cash left after recent celebrations, is indicated this evening.

6. FRIDAY

Financial matters that have been troubling you ease a little as a result of something that happens today, but schemes for wide-ranging domestic improvements will have to be kept on hold until a treasure ship comes in. If you've been considering a career move, be sure to keep a lunchtime appointment, however inconvenient. You are letting thoughts of prestige and status influence you too much in a personal relationship.

7. SATURDAY

You'll sleep late and wake hoping for a lazy day. You won't get it, because a big family gathering is indicated. The morning will be spent shopping to feed the hungry hordes; the afternoon cooking and serving the goodies. Older guests and younger people will have different ideas about entertainment, which could cause an argument. Don't link up with another Fish tonight, or you've had your chips!

8. SUNDAY

There's clearing up to do this morning, in more ways than one. After helping a partner with a dirty job, you have to deal with a telephone call from an angry relative. Either you forgot to invite them to your home, or ignored them when they arrived. Make your apologies at least *sound* convincing. If neighbours had to put up with noise last night, ask them round for a drink in order to smooth over any ill feelings.

9. MONDAY

Although you have high hopes of a new work partnership, it gets off to a bad start. Remember that Pisceans are supposed to be generous and forgiving, not grasping and overbearing, and you will be able to retrieve the situation. Go with the flow in a social situation: a show of independence will not be appreciated. It will be an evening when you'll be happiest at home, reading or doing a hobby.

10. TUESDAY

Some say Pisceans are lazy, but today you blaze with energy. You're the ringmaster in life's circus now, but try not to crack your whip too loudly at work or at home, or you'll be branded a bossy boots! If you have to drive tonight, take a good road map: you'll find yourself in unfamiliar surroundings and possibly in fog. Your romantic prospects seem misty too, and the stars can shed little light on them.

11. WEDNESDAY

Keep your ear to the ground and you'll be able to keep one step ahead of events all day. Your inside information will come from a colleague of the opposite sex. Read between the lines in a business letter and you will see the way towards a lucrative deal. Don't try to manipulate people; workmates will withdraw their support if they feel you're trying to use them to feather your own nest.

12. THURSDAY

A turbulent day, when you won't know whether you're on your arm (to put it politely) or your elbow. An important piece of domestic equipment will conk out. An impulse buy will turn out to be the worst bargain you've made for weeks. A relationship you thought was stable will shake like a grass skirt in a hurricane. You'll pig out on chocolate to cheer yourself up – and think about buying an exercise bike tomorrow!

13. FRIDAY

You will have a good day if you share what you have with others. The things most in demand are your knowledge and your time. A workmate who envies a particular skill you have will become a good friend if you pass it on to them. Later, a child will need help with an educational project. It will involve a library trip that will eat into time you had earmarked for relaxation, but you'll find out what they need to know.

14. SATURDAY

Let friends plan your day, for you are short of ideas now, while they are in top form. Their advice will be to let domestic tasks slide and go out on the town. You've worked hard over the last few days – so why not? However, if a partner comes with you, beware of showing too much admiration for an attractive stranger. You will probably have dinner in luxurious surroundings. Never mind the bill, you're being given a treat.

15. SUNDAY

Although the weather may be bad, make a point of getting out of the house as soon as you've completed unavoidable chores. You could meet pleasant people who share your interests at a concert or an exhibition of craft work. On a more intimate level, you are trying to hide something from a partner. Bring it out into the open now; if they find out the secret from a third person it could destroy all the trust between you.

16. MONDAY

Much as you might like to be, you are not one of nature's revolutionaries. This morning you will be bored at the prospect of the same old pattern at work. However, you will be the one who makes the most fuss when a change in routine is suddenly announced. Calm down: the new arrangement will prove to be to your advantage. It may result in a slight reduction in your working hours, with no financial penalty.

17. TUESDAY

Take care with correspondence, or you will make a commitment it will be difficult to honour. Someone will try to bully you into making a decision. Resist them, and if necessary call on a friend who owes you a favour for support. A social gathering in an uninhibited club or pub will give young, unattached Pisceans a chance to do some talent-spotting tonight. Don't sow any wild oats; you won't welcome the harvest!

18. WEDNESDAY

Don't push your luck today. That charm you're wearing doesn't guarantee that you can take silly risks and escape unscathed. Pay special attention to this advice if you're driving. A so-called friend will betray your trust, and not for the first time. Resolve to turn your back on them for good. Money can't buy you love, so don't waste it on an expensive treat for someone who doesn't return your feelings.

19. THURSDAY

A problem that arises at home in the morning will haunt you throughout the day. Don't let it make you absent-minded at work, or you will make a costly mistake. Keep your temper when a workmate teases you. If you start a quarrel, it will go much further than you intended. Your time and sympathy, rather than your physical passion, are needed now to mend a rift that has developed in a close personal relationship.

20. FRIDAY

A financial worry may have given you a sleepless night, and you will feel washed out this morning. You will only make things harder for yourself if you refuse to discuss monetary problems with a partner. They will gladly offer support if you will only ask for it. Be firm when a gossiping neighbour invades your home and outstays their welcome. Don't tangle with a Taurean tonight, or you'll end up taking a fall.

21. SATURDAY

A long-cherished ambition can be realized. It is connected with a sporting skill; possibly it's the first time you'll negotiate a ski slope without a tumble! However, someone else will have one: a child will require first-aid attention after a minor mishap. If romantic troubles have been making you blue, something that happens tonight will put colour back into your cheeks – but it may be red, from blushing!

22. SUNDAY

You will have a golden opportunity to rid yourself of a burden or restriction that has weighed you down for too long. It could be an over-demanding acquaintance, an interfering relative, or a piece of equipment that has let you down one time too many. Whatever it is, kick it out! In a personal relationship, beware of showing too much sympathy for a lame duck, or you will saddle yourself with another burden.

23. MONDAY

Your unworldly Piscean nature means that certain relationships often present you with problems; this is especially true when you are confronted by aggressive people. Today, however, when you witness an act of cruelty, you will have no hesitation in facing down a bully. Your victory will much improve your social standing. After this excitement, you'll relish a quiet evening at home with your loved ones.

24. TUESDAY

Work goes slowly: you know just what you need to do, but you have difficulty doing it. A long midday break will help recharge your batteries. It will cheer you up, too, when you buy a 'by-gone' that its seller has undervalued. Later, things will run more smoothly. Young Pisceans beginning a romantic relationship should take it easy. Concentrate on laying strong foundations on which to build later.

25. WEDNESDAY

You will disagree with a close friend over a money-making scheme in which you have both been involved. Make it clear to them that you will no longer turn a blind eye to their dubious dealings. It may be the best thing for both of you to bring your long association to an end. Tonight you'll want to spend some time alone thinking things over, but your partner may not understand your desire for solitude.

26. THURSDAY

No, you are not paranoid – someone really is out to get you at work, and a tactless remark you make this morning could give them fresh ammunition. Guard your tongue all day. Happily, something that happens around lunchtime will allow you to throw a spanner in their works. A powerful ally will appear to support you. Something you see on television tonight will give you a burning desire to acquire a new skill.

27. FRIDAY

An organizational change this morning makes your working environment more agreeable. You've been overspending lately; now it's time to think of saving for a rainy day. An unexpected expense connected with travel is indicated: maybe you should get the car serviced very soon! You may be feeling unloved. It's all in your mind: take a good look around you and you'll find that someone is waiting.

28. SATURDAY

All kinds of communal activity are well starred today. So it's a fine time to reach out and make contact with people who share your beliefs and aims. You may do this at a social club, in a political organization, or as a member of a creative or artistic group. Later, your mind will be put at rest in a romantic matter. If you make your intentions clear to a lover, you will get a warm and welcoming response.

29. SUNDAY

The disturbing dreams you had last night may have been prophetic, for dramas and difficulties will plague your personal life today. You realize that you have upset your partner or family in some way, but when you question them, no one is prepared to give you a straight answer. Sit tight and wait; all will be made clear soon. Take care when making a short, routine journey: accidents will happen when they're least expected.

30. MONDAY

Patience and caution will be necessary at work,
where a disagreement will arise over a duty
schedule. It will be up to you to make an offer to
bury the hatchet, in order to end an estrangement
from a colleague of the opposite sex. Unattached
Pisceans can now afford to play hard to get. You'll
get plenty of offers if you're on the romantic market,
but if you sit tight for a while your value will rocket!

31. TUESDAY

Make it clear to a partner or business associate that
you are tired of arguments and lengthy discussions
over a proposed plan. If a deal is to be made, it must
be struck now. Otherwise the project is off. You will
find that a domestic improvement is going to cost
far more than you budgeted for, but you will decide
that it must be done. Repulse a selfish lover who
will try to take advantage of your Piscean generosity.

FEBRUARY

1. WEDNESDAY

This will be a generally dull day, but you will be able
to take boredom in your stride, for something that
happens will help stabilize your financial position.
Spend the day considering how you can break out of
stale patterns and avoid repeating past mistakes.
The way forward may seem far from clear. In fact,
the stars are doing you a favour by making you slow
down and reconsider your priorities.

2. THURSDAY

In contrast to yesterday, your creative thought
undergoes a power surge. Colleagues are eager to
listen to your suggestions and plans, and quick to
agree to them. Anyone who tries to give you the
run-around will find that your stamina outlasts
them. In personal relationships, too, all
confrontations today will work out in your favour.
Any romantic difficulties will be temporary and
trivial setbacks.

3. FRIDAY

A telephone call this morning will send you dashing
off on a journey. Take full advantage of any money-
making opportunity you are offered at your
destination, especially if it is somehow connected
with tourism. All kinds of possibilities may arise,
and you are well placed to make the most of them.
However, don't let personal likes or dislikes
influence your decisions, or excellent chances will
go begging.

4. SATURDAY

Don't wait for fate to take a hand today; take the lead in shaping life to your advantage. You must assert yourself now if you are to be given the respect that you deserve. You will make it clear to a partner that you are no longer prepared to put up with unrealistic financial demands. You must be tough, also, with associates who have for too long taken your loyalty and generosity for granted.

5. SUNDAY

An annoying task faces you this morning, when you will have to fill out a complex form, connected with taxes or another financial matter. Later, a walk in woodland will blow away the bureaucratic cobwebs. You will have to control your temper when you are embarrassed by a friend's outrageous behaviour in a public place. Don't be too soft-hearted with an errant lover or your illusions will soon be shattered.

6. MONDAY

A letter that comes this morning will remind you of an old love affair. Don't get all misty-eyed: burn it and quickly forget it. Your current romantic partnership needs all your attention now. If you've been thinking of changing your job, this could be the day you attend a crucial interview. If you're looking for employment, close attention to the small ads in a local newspaper will pay off.

7. TUESDAY

Others will give you a hard time today if you provide them with an opening. Tread carefully, for you will be liable to misunderstand other people's intentions and to over-estimate your own powers of dealing with them. Don't rely on intuition or hunches to guide you; stick to the facts. In romantic relationships, young Pisceans will be thinking of tearing up their roots and finding fresh fields to frolic in.

8. WEDNESDAY

Be sure not to let an unfortunate experience in the past get in the way of a promising new development in your working life. What happens today may mark a high point in your working year, and can greatly improve your financial position. In the personal sphere, you will suspect that a close friend is speaking with a forked tongue. Be quick to nail a lie if you detect one, even if it means ending the relationship.

9. THURSDAY

A craving for public recognition of your talents could lead you astray today. If you go fishing for compliments, no one will take the bait. Don't start a witch-hunt for secret enemies; they are phantoms of your imagination. Remember that domestic happiness is equally as important to you as career success, and turn to your nearest and dearest for the support that is now essential to your wellbeing.

10. FRIDAY

Shake off a crisis of confidence this morning, and you will be able to make good progress in routine tasks. Just don't attempt anything too ambitious. Any problems you encounter will be as a result of your own lack of confidence; tell yourself you can tackle them, and they will melt away. An outing planned for the evening will have to be cancelled because of unforeseen circumstances.

11. SATURDAY

You'll feel the need for exercise to burn off the energy that floods you this morning. Don't overtax yourself and risk a strain: a half-mile jog may suit you better than a half-marathon. Your glow of wellbeing will light up a social gathering tonight, when a get-together with folk outside your usual circle will be rewarding. You'll meet new people and exchange exciting ideas.

12. SUNDAY

Short of moving to another planet, there's no way you'll escape from other people, so you will just have to make the best of their vile moods now. You'd be happier alone – but meanwhile be happy that you're alive, because if hard words and harder looks could kill, you'd be long gone. However, they won't attack unprovoked, so if you retire deep into your shell, you'll survive. It won't be safe to come out until tomorrow.

13. MONDAY

As befits a Piscean, you will pay more attention to spiritual values today than to career or financial considerations. You will be given the chance to make a sizeable material gain by underhand means. All you have to do is betray a colleague. If you give way to temptation, you will feel empty and disillusioned when the first thrill of success wears off. You will find that a clear conscience is a greater prize.

14. TUESDAY

You won't be able to duck responsibilities, so don't waste time trying. Any excuses you make to get out of obligations will be swiftly exposed as bogus. The efforts you are forced to make will stretch you to the utmost, but you'll get your jobs done. There will be a financial bonus, as well as praise from a partner. By the way, that Valentine did not come for the person that you think it did!

15. WEDNESDAY

Although a domestic problem is on your mind, you must summon up all your self-control in order to concentrate on your career. You will question the wisdom of entering into a financial transaction with someone you are quite unable to understand. A word with a mutual acquaintance will help you to make up your mind. Don't let a social obligation tonight make you neglect the needs of a long-term partner.

16. THURSDAY

A telephone call this morning will remove uncertainties that have been hanging over a business or social relationship. If you're lunching out, look for a casual acquaintance wearing a green or blue scarf; they may not know it, but they have information of interest to you. An unfamiliar sporting activity is indicated for the evening, when your skill may surprise your friends as much as it does you.

17. FRIDAY

There are times when you'd rather be the nail than the hammer. This is one of them. You will long for colleagues or partners to take the lead in a baffling situation. You'll have to swallow your pride and yell for help before it is forthcoming. If you go on trying to suppress your feelings for a certain person, you will blow your mind. Speak out now, and get the matter settled one way or another.

18. SATURDAY

You will be worrying over something you said last night. Perhaps you should not have spoken so bluntly; but things said cannot be unsaid, and you'll just waste time if you go on agonizing about it. If you have children, they will do much to restore your peace of mind today. If not, you could find relaxation in childish pastimes: a jigsaw puzzle would give you something to do with your hands.

19. SUNDAY

Whatever you've been doing to wear yourself out, stop it now! You have a chance to relax; if you do not take it you risk a stress-related ailment. Let your partner deal with a neighbour who comes to complain about the behaviour of children or pets. This evening, put on some soothing music and lie back in a nice warm bath. Afterwards you will find love with your partner as it was really meant to be experienced.

20. MONDAY

If you've delayed a decision to make a commitment, whether work-related, financial, or emotional, you now get the go-ahead signal. It's a time for finalizing agreements, signing contracts, or forging lasting personal ties. You've been sceptical about certain promises made to you, but now you find they were sincere. You'll want to celebrate: a table for two will be more enjoyable than a noisy party.

21. TUESDAY

Make haste slowly: any progress today will come from steady, methodical work. You'll be inclined to go along with other people's suggestions, simply because you haven't the stamina to oppose them. Is your physical condition all that it should be? An improvement in your diet, and regular, gentle exercise, would give you greater reserves of energy. Tonight, a Lion may put back the bite in your romantic life.

22. WEDNESDAY

The less you attempt, the more you'll achieve. Over-ambitious schemes will be shot down in flames by more practical associates, but sensible suggestions for small-scale improvements will be warmly received. Later, things will get difficult unless you can exert some self-control. Suppress your urge to go over the top, or you will find yourself out on a limb, and someone waiting to chop it off!

23. THURSDAY

An improvement in conditions and the good humour of colleagues will make the workplace pleasant and stimulating. You will spend a good deal of time dealing with members of the public; probably advising rather than selling. The lunch-break gives you a chance to iron out a personal misunderstanding. Spontaneous and uncritical reactions to a new outfit will win you extra affection from a partner this evening.

24. FRIDAY

When chaos threatens to rule today, adopt an independent attitude and be as adaptable as possible. Then you will escape the panic-bug that appears to have bitten your colleagues. You will win the approval of superiors by remaining calm while workmates run around like headless chickens. Later, in a dimly-lit setting, you'll be bitten by the lovebug – or perhaps nipped by a Crab!

25. SATURDAY

Try not to make waves this morning: a partner is in an edgy mood. Suppress any aggrieved feelings, and be on your guard against careless remarks. You will be blamed for a breakage that occurs in the kitchen. Things lighten up later, when all the family will enjoy a trip to a natural beauty spot. Tonight you'll have had enough of being Captain Sensible, and you'll get an opportunity to indulge one of your zaniest urges.

26. SUNDAY

People blow hot and cold today, and their sudden mood changes will baffle and irritate you. You'll be forced to lay down the law with a partner who has pushed their luck once too often. Difficulty in securing emotional support from friends will force you to fall back upon your own inner strengths. Happily, they will be enough to tide you through. The only thing you'll get to cuddle tonight is your hot-water bottle.

27. MONDAY

Your mood will change rapidly: at one moment you want to conquer the world; the next you'd be happy to settle down in a cosy armchair. Try to channel your bursts of energy into productive projects. This would be a good time to re-think your wardrobe; after all, spring is on the way! At a social function tonight, a person of a kind you wouldn't normally look at twice will prove strangely fascinating.

28. TUESDAY

Congratulate yourself, you lucky little Fish, if this is
your birthday. It's a particularly favourable one,
indicating that you can expect many goodies to
come your way for the rest of the year. Any that
arrive today, you might like to share with your less
fortunate Piscean friends born in a Leap Year, on 29
February. Some of your luck may rub off on to them,
but you have plenty to spare.

MARCH

1. WEDNESDAY

Avoid strenuous physical activity: your agility rating is low, and you risk a strain. However, your brain is working nimbly enough, and you will win praise for a good piece of work this morning. Your sensitivity to fashion is at its height, too, so this would be a good day to shop for a new outfit. Amateur dramatics take up much of your evening, when you may also take a starring role in a personal drama.

2. THURSDAY

Any recent arguments should be settled under the influences of today's peaceful stars. You can resolve a difference with a colleague without betraying your principles. In a problem where you must set personal feelings against financial considerations, you will be ruled by your heart rather than your head. Take a partner's advice concerning a joint venture that is proposed to you.

3. FRIDAY

It will be a mistake to take offence when an associate criticizes you. Their observations are fair and are meant to be helpful; only your Piscean sensitivity makes you take them the wrong way. You will escape further criticism if you reorganize your working or social life along more sensible lines. Beware of a loud-mouthed Aquarian who will try to drive a wedge between you and your partner.

4. SATURDAY

Some lucky Pisceans will find themselves on a winter sports' holiday. If you're one of them, stay to well-beaten tracks today; snow conditions are treacherous. If you're at home, creative pursuits, especially painting and embroidery, will give most satisfaction. In either case, relationships with partners are harmonious. The unattached will find multiple flirtations harmless and stimulating.

5. SUNDAY

Lack of cash will clip your wings when you feel a surge of wanderlust. You'd like to take off into the wild blue yonder, but you've hardly got the price of a bus ticket to the park! You could console yourself by going over the plans you've made for your summer holiday, but you will get more satisfaction from reading material on further education you received recently. There is a study course just made for you.

6. MONDAY

Certain changes that occur now mean that your work routine will increasingly intrude into your social life. Some commitments will have to be rearranged, but make up your mind not to allow any outside influence to undermine a close personal relationship. In a discussion on joint financial arrangements, make sure that others have no cause to complain that you are trying to shirk any responsibilities.

7. TUESDAY

In your Piscean day-dreaming, do you sometimes see yourself as James Bond or Modesty Blaise? You may need to be an action hero(ine) today, when a business or social journey becomes an adventure. You are first on the scene at an accident. Stay cool, act fast, and don't forget your first-aid drill. Afterwards, you may have to leave in a hurry if you want to escape the attentions of local media reporters.

8. WEDNESDAY

More changes at work are indicated, but you will easily adapt to them. Communications with colleagues and partners are good, so it's a fine time to put forward new ideas. Diplomacy will be needed in a business meeting: blunt and tactless speaking could harm your career prospects. Later, you'll come out unscathed from a potentially dangerous confrontation if you can manage to make people laugh at themselves.

9. THURSDAY

Your carelessness will cause minor damage to a colleague's property. They make a fuss, and you can't solve the problem by throwing money at it. Even though you feel it's a storm in a tea-cup, a full apology will be needed. Keep clear of a conspiracy among your acquaintances: the trick they are planning to play is just not funny. Tonight you will find that variety is the spice of love-life.

10. FRIDAY

Don't miss out on an opportunity to strike a hard bargain. Your special skills are in demand, and you should sell them to the highest bidder. Take no notice of a person who tries to belittle you: they are driven by envy, as other people well know. Someone is gazing adoringly at you from a distance – but you won't know anything about it until they come close enough to see the whites of your eyes!

11. SATURDAY

Did you remember to lock up the house tightly last night? The stars say that a police officer is on the way to your home, and the indications are that you may have suffered a break-in. You'll be caused more annoyance than material loss – and you'll pay more attention to domestic security in future. A friend who comes to sympathize tonight will give you advice that will help with an emergency repair job.

12. SUNDAY

You can relax now, the excitement's over for the time being. You will be offered a 'genuine antique' for a low price at a car boot or jumble sale. It may look ugly and battered, but snap it up! Get an expert's opinion as soon as possible, and you could be pleasantly surprised. A partner has been cool recently, but now the magic comes back into your relationship. Forget domestic chores and get to bed early!

13. MONDAY

Another particularly well-starred Piscean birthday!
If you haven't taken a day off to celebrate, you'll
need to deal with urgent correspondence and
routine tasks, but then you will put aside workaday
worries and make merry. Treating friends will be
expensive at lunchtime. You'll have a great party
tonight, although there may be an embarrassing
moment when a jilted lover attempts to get their
own back with a snide comment!

14. TUESDAY

Whether or not a certain situation develops to your
advantage will depend entirely on the attitude you
take. If you are true to Pisces' saintly traits and take
a high-minded approach, you will get the best of it.
Sneaky behaviour will bring failure. In an argument
with a loved one, be assertive rather than aggressive,
but make it clear that you will not let their selfish
motives tie you down to the past.

15. WEDNESDAY

Letter-writing, telephone calls and other
communications will dominate your day. A travel
plan will have to be altered at the last moment, so
be sure that any documents concerned are amended.
Later, you will try to restrain a partner who has
ambitious plans for home redecoration. It isn't a
matter of expense; you just don't share their taste in
furnishings. Better be tactful as you state your case.

16. THURSDAY

Faced with a financial problem, you'll find you have cause to give thanks for a caring network of friends. Lunchtime brings the chance to improve your image: perhaps you should have your hair seen to? Home life tonight centres on the kitchen: you'll be cooking, or eating, an unfamiliar dish. Young Pisceans looking for romance will remember a culinary motto: 'If you can't stand the heat, get out of the kitchen'!

17. FRIDAY

You may be absent from work today; in any case, the stars indicate that you have very little to do. For once you can indulge in the favourite Piscean pastime of day-dreaming. However, don't make the mistake of thinking that your wildest dreams are about to come true. You will begin to think that a new romantic partner is your ideal mate. You are certainly in tune physically, but disharmony will arise elsewhere.

18. SATURDAY

Being born on the cusp proves lucky today, when Pisceans celebrating a birthday can expect an especially good year ahead. You'll find security and satisfaction in love. Your celebrations appear to involve psychic trappings: be very wary of accepting any 'messages' that come through when playing with a ouija board. Forceful persuasion will be necessary to get rid of an uninvited and unpleasant guest.

19. SUNDAY

A recent birthday started you thinking about the
shape you're in. If you feel you're looking older than
your calendar age, begin to roll back the years now.
Diet and exercise are the tools. Put some spring into
spring by joining a health club or taking up a sport.
Golf is great for either sex at any age, and would
widen your social circle. Tonight, a partner may
convince you that you're not as old as you feel.

20. MONDAY

You will need to stand up to an overbearing
colleague who tries to lay down the law. Your luck
looks good, so buy a raffle ticket if one's on offer. A
modest flutter on a horse ridden by a jockey with an
Irish name will pay off. It may also be worth
investing in a share issue tipped by a business
contact. An illicit affair will be brought out into the
open as a result of a friend's indiscreet remarks.

21. TUESDAY

The morning post brings news of a financial
windfall of some kind; it may be an inheritance from
a distant relative. Ironically, your closer family is
likely to be the cause of considerable expense today.
Good fortune is indicated for anyone involved in
property deals, whether buying or selling. If you're
thinking of making a move, this will be a good day
for viewing a new house or showing your own.

22. WEDNESDAY

You don't like to doubt others' good faith, but today you must be sceptical. Don't believe everything you are told, even by your nearest and dearest. If you give credit to unpleasant rumours, whatever their source, unnecessary fears will cloud your mind. You may think that a colleague is trying to undermine your position. This is the not the case; they are just trying to protect their own interests.

23. THURSDAY

Organization is your strongest suit today. If you find yourself loaded with work, you can easily and safely delegate it to colleagues. That way you'll save energy that you can spend on those you love. A creative idea, possibly connected with fashion, may promise monetary gain. You are in the limelight socially. Something you do or say at a function will provoke gossip, but you don't need to worry about it.

24. FRIDAY

They didn't know you had it in you! This will be the reaction of friends or colleagues when you reveal an unexpected skill. Even you will be surprised at your achievement, and it may decide you to revive an old ambition. Another result may be an appearance on a local radio or television show. Come clean about your intentions in a romantic situation tonight, or a lover will try to play dirty!

25. SATURDAY

You'll be tempted to throw a wobbly when a child misbehaves this morning. Keep your cool and listen to their excuses: you may find that sympathy, not scolding, is needed. An article lost long ago will come to light in an unexpected place. You'll have cause to congratulate a friend who comes with news of a new job. Fancy-free Pisceans could begin a long-lasting relationship with a gentle Goat tonight.

26. SUNDAY

Today will be romantic and lighthearted. You don't need to take life too seriously, so take the chance to be adventurous: explore new places and meet interesting people. A trip to a nearby city is indicated. A suggestion made by a new acquaintance could help you in a career move. Don't try too hard to reform a lover who has a wandering eye; that may be one of the main points of their attraction.

27. MONDAY

A plan long nurtured in secret – for financial or family reasons – must be put into action now, or it will have no chance of success. Your enthusiasm will capture the imaginations of others, and you will win their support. Although they will offer good advice, you will have to do most of the work yourself. It will put pressure on your domestic and social life, but the financial results are likely to be substantial.

28. TUESDAY

Commuters will experience long delays this morning. You will feel a craving for knowledge. Make inquiries about the possibility of attending a study course that would further your career. If you're permanently employed, you might get time off for such a purpose. You may find yourself powerfully drawn towards a work superior. On no account must you make the first approach – if one is to be made at all.

29. WEDNESDAY

There is more trouble with transport today when you are likely to find yourself stranded by the non-appearance of a bus or train, or the breakdown of a car. You could miss an important business or social appointment. On the plus side, your finances are boosted by a gift or long-term loan from an older relative. You will refuse to play ball with an avid Aquarian who challenges you to a game of love.

30. THURSDAY

In contrast to recent days, travel is now well starred. All journeys you take today will run smoothly, and you will be warmly received wherever you go. You can rely on your instincts in making any decisions. Although it's often a recipe for disaster, it will do no harm today if you let your romantic emotions influence you in a business matter. People you love have exciting plans for your entertainment tonight.

31. FRIDAY

You will find a new way to express your
individuality, probably through contact with a
foreign country or a person of a different race. Don't
neglect routine tasks; you will accomplish
constructive work towards long-term goals if you
keep your mind to it. It is a make-or-break time in
romantic relationships. Tonight could see the
revival of a flagging love affair, or the beginning of a
new one.

APRIL

1. SATURDAY

Would-be pranksters will find that there are no flies on you this morning, but don't shoo them away too impatiently, or you'll be branded a sour-puss. If you're a member of one of the caring professions, as many Pisceans are, you may have to answer an emergency call this afternoon. Altogether, you have a serious day – and that's all the more reason to beware of making yourself a fool for love tonight.

2. SUNDAY

Beware of jumping to conclusions about a partner's motives: what you see as unfair pressure, they may regard as helpful guidance. In any case, this is a time when it will be best to let others sit in the driver's seat. This is true both figuratively and literally: your judgement of distances will be poor today, and you could have a crunch when trying to park a car. Keep the evening free for relaxation.

3. MONDAY

Knock on the right door at the right moment, and you will open a gateway to opportunity. You will need to ask a favour from someone in authority if you are to fulfil a business or domestic ambition. Good judgement, in asking the right person, and accurate timing, in asking at the right moment, will determine whether or not your request is granted. If it is, you can expect to be travelling to far places soon.

4. TUESDAY

A money-making opportunity that arises this morning will deserve serious consideration. Don't be influenced by the opinions and prejudices of your closest associates. Make up your own mind, after carefully weighing up the characters of the people you will have to work with if you accept. Don't have any doubts about your sex appeal now, or nervousness will have a bad effect on your most intimate relationships.

5. WEDNESDAY

A past effort will be rewarded with increased leisure time today. You use it to put certain personal affairs in order. Devote attention to your most prized possessions: insure valuable objects, for some future loss is indicated. Get expert advice on a contract or credit agreement that is puzzling you. A walk down memory lane, alone or with an old friend, will fill your evening.

6. THURSDAY

Employers or superiors are conscious of your desire for new challenges and responsibilities, and today they will give you the chance to shine. It may well involve travel. You don't need to worry about dressing to kill: your charm and wit will impress any people you meet so much that they won't notice if you are wearing a potato sack! Someone you encounter in 'horsy' surroundings may set your pulses steeple-chasing.

7. FRIDAY

Again there are indications of opportunities to travel and benefits from new contacts in far places. You will find that you have a great deal in common with a person of a different race or colour. They could become important both to your career and in your personal life. At home, a property transaction may seem fraught with difficulty and uncertainty. The outcome will remain unclear until the end of the month.

8. SATURDAY

This is a good day to experiment with your image. If you're shopping for clothes, be adventurous in your choice, and don't be swayed by the opinions of older friends or relatives. A 'new you' could attract welcome attention at a social function tonight. Solo Pisceans will find that the chemistry seems to be right in a new relationship – but don't make any wild experiments or you'll raise a stink!

9. SUNDAY

You will need to pay extra attention to a partner, who will wake you today by singing the blues very loudly. Think fast of a way to cheer them up: volunteering to take over irksome domestic duties for the day will help. A visit from a favourite relative later may help to take some of the pressure off. The evening promises to be boring, but you'll think of an original way to put some life into it.

10. MONDAY

A wish could come true, but only if you conquer an inclination to waste time, and go all out in pursuit of it. If you are still considering a recent financial opportunity or job offer, this is your last chance to make up your mind. You must give more thought to your emotional development, and resolve to be less selfish in certain ways, if you are now thinking of entering into a permanent relationship with a lover.

11. TUESDAY

Success today will depend upon whom you choose to help you. Business and romantic partnerships are of equal importance, so now is the time to choose wisely. With the right support, you can afford to aim high. You can also afford a shopping trip, when you should be on the lookout for bargains in electrical goods. A close friend who has been having marital problems will telephone this evening with good news.

12. WEDNESDAY

If you've been waiting for the right time to persuade certain people to support a pet project, this is it. You will still encounter some opposition, but the people who count will be on your side. Later, you will be preoccupied by childhood memories, and will rake up something in your past you would rather forget. A chance meeting tonight could become very significant in the light of future events.

13. THURSDAY

Be true to your conscience, when influential people try to force you to say or do something against your will. If you let yourself be pushed around, or compromise in the hope of material gain, you will bitterly regret it in the future. Stick to the jobs you are most familiar with: it is a bad time to tackle anything new. That applies in romantic matters, too; familiar partners are better than new attachments.

14. FRIDAY

Decisions taken jointly will be more successful than those made alone. You may be under pressure to make changes in social arrangements. Misunderstandings are likely, and appointments may have to be cancelled, if everyone concerned is not kept fully informed of your movements. You've long suspected that the perfect partner doesn't exist, but someone you meet now may make you think again.

15. SATURDAY

If you're thinking of moving house, you could find your ideal home today. Those who are staying put will have exciting ideas for redecorating their present residence. Family and friends will be pleased to give a hand with do-it-yourself efforts – but watch out for a colour-blind relative! Congratulate a friend who wins a prize you'd hoped for, and some of their good luck will rub off on you.

16. SUNDAY

You are full of new ideas about practically everything today, but perhaps you would do better to keep them to yourself. If you scatter your enthusiasm around like a dog's breakfast, you will find yourself left alone to clear up the mess. However, you'll find it impossible to stop telling others what they should do. The force of your personality could empty rooms today, and it almost certainly will!

17. MONDAY

Everyone will be attracted by your restful quality today, so make the most of your ability to put people at their ease. It's a good time for business meetings, when agreements will be easily reached. In your personal life, however, you'll decide you will have to be more selfish in a certain matter if things are to be put in order. A laughing Lion met in a den of iniquity (or a new club) may tickle your fancy.

18. TUESDAY

Money worries rear their ugly heads. You may have to inspect your most valuable possessions with a view to selling some of them. If this becomes necessary, be sure to have any art objects or jewellery valued by an expert before deciding on your asking price. A friend will have a helpful suggestion to improve your bank balance. It's not a time to take chances: don't do anything for a dare or a bet tonight.

19. WEDNESDAY

You will be faced with an embarrassing task. A friend or colleague, well liked in every other way, has a problem with 'bodily freshness'. It could be easily solved with a new shampoo or deodorant. Telling them will be an unpleasant job, but for their own good someone has to do it – and you're the one elected. Later, a meeting with a business contact may prove to be more romantic than either of you expected.

20. THURSDAY

An especially good day for any Piscean belonging to an ethnic minority in the community where they live. You'll receive very good news from your own or your ancestors' country of origin, probably involving financial gain. A religious problem that has caused some concern will be solved to the satisfaction of all concerned. A traditional approach in a romantic matter will bring the best results.

21. FRIDAY

You are feeling talkative, but it would be better to listen rather than lecture. Be quiet, and you'll learn something of advantage to you. You'll slip up in a business deal if you approach it with too much feeling and not enough thought. You will find yourself unexpectedly alone this evening, when friends let you down at the last moment. Take the chance to settle down with a good book or some restful music.

22. SATURDAY

Sherlock Holmes is your new name, and when you go out investigating today, you'll find out something that others would rather keep to themselves. Don't spread the secret around, or you'll get into deep trouble. Later, your imagination is likely to play tricks on you. You won't believe what a friend appears to be up to – and you'll be right not to believe it. Save your fantasies for use in a loving context tonight.

23. SUNDAY

An older relative will ask your advice on a personal matter. Don't give a definite answer until you are sure you've got all the facts straight. Putting your feet up will be the most sensible thing you can do this afternoon; you've had a hard week, so you'll resist the family's clamour for an outing. Make it up to them with a treat this evening: everyone would probably enjoy an exotic takeaway dinner.

24. MONDAY

You'll make a promising start to a job this morning – but then a sudden lack of confidence will make you botch it up. Start again, and this time don't be afraid to ask for the help of a more experienced colleague. You will also tend to be clumsy: watch out when handling fragile objects. Be careful what you say tonight, when tactlessness in a social situation could embarrass and alienate a very important person.

25. TUESDAY

You will have to make a painful decision in order to make the best of an irretrievable situation. You must decide to cut your losses and begin again. Later, you'll move back into the fast lane. You'll stop worrying about what everyone else is doing, and concentrate on what you can do. Unattached Pisceans will find that what has seemed to be an endless period of loss and heartache is now coming to an end.

26. WEDNESDAY

A misunderstanding will cause frustration this morning. You will know exactly what you want to say, but the words come out all wrong. Give your tongue a rest, while you concentrate on getting routine tasks up to date. A friend's tips on health and nutrition will be worth hearing – and acting upon. Male Pisceans take warning: your attentions will not be welcomed if you try to force them on a shy Virgoan.

27. THURSDAY

Self-discipline is necessary. There will be many demands on your Piscean generosity, and you must steel yourself to turn down some requests. You must put your own needs first today. If you overload your schedule now you will risk a burn-out. If you're feeling stressed later, try to relax with a practical hobby or intellectual interest. Your romantic life will certainly improve if you tell a partner a few home truths.

28. FRIDAY

Your schedule today will be varied and adventurous, and you may visit places you have never been to before. You will be tempted to buy a shockingly expensive and utterly outrageous article of clothing – but if you really want strangers to turn their heads as you pass by, it would be cheaper to dye your hair bright green! Solo Pisceans could find that plans to spend the weekend with a lover are suddenly cancelled.

29. SATURDAY

It promises to be a quiet day, but a telephone call may point the way to an exciting trip in the very near future. You will win praise by solving a domestic problem that is baffling your partner or family. Try to make friends a part of any entertainment you plan for later in the day; their ideas for fun will be better than yours. For solo Pisceans, silver speech will create the possibility of sexual magic.

30. SUNDAY

You feel like a change of scene, so you'll visit relatives or friends whom you haven't seen for a while. You will have your midday meal in a place which holds very special memories for you. You will get the chance to help an older relation who has been going through a difficult, lonely period. Spend the evening catching up on neglected correspondence: someone out there is longing to hear your latest news.

MAY

1. MONDAY

You have put off making a decision on a financial problem for far too long. Today you will be forced to act, and you may find you have to break a tie with the past in order to give your new budget a chance to succeed. Take a career opportunity that comes your way without hesitation, and don't be afraid to make a binding agreement. You will create bad feeling if you are over-critical of a friend or partner's artistic efforts.

2. TUESDAY

The day begins pleasantly with the arrival of an unexpected gift. You should write a thank-you letter immediately, or the sender will be upset. It's a good time to talk to a superior or business adviser about a recent financial decision. Later, you will be full of nervous energy, and a partner's inactivity may begin to annoy you. Turn your attention to some constructive activity, or you will start a row.

3. WEDNESDAY

If you have recently entered a competition, you could have good news today. You will not at first recognize something that happens now as a major turning point in your business or social life, but it will later prove to be so. It may be connected with an honour or award given for work in the community. Beware of jealousy and over-possessiveness if you want a current romantic relationship to continue to prosper.

4. THURSDAY

Cultivate an optimistic frame of mind, and you will make a good impression on everyone you meet today. They will find it hard to deny you any reasonable request. You will benefit if you take a chance to introduce a business associate to members of your family. Single Pisceans will be embarrassed when a secret affair is suddenly brought out into the open, but the consequences will not be as serious as you fear.

5. FRIDAY

Recent financial pressures ease now, but not for long if you fail to restrain your urge towards extravagance. Easy come, easy go, seems to be your attitude. If you must spend money today, buy something that will beautify your home environment: you could get an original painting for the price of the unnecessary gadget that you have your eye on! A romantic dinner for two tonight may end up by giving you indigestion!

6. SATURDAY

The indications are that you will attend a conference or reunion today. Whether you're doing high-powered deals with business people, or simply catching up with the gossip of old schoolfriends, you'll have an enjoyable time. A friend may suggest you try yoga or meditation to relieve stress. A partnership can be retrieved from almost certain disaster if you now go all out to demonstrate your love and loyalty.

7. SUNDAY

Since you're in the mood for change, this would be a good day to consider redecorating your home, or going through your wardrobe to see what should be discarded or replaced. Since you're feeling energetic, take the chance to repay recent hospitality. You've spent quite a bit of time in friends' homes lately, so tonight invite them round to your place for a rave-up – or coffee and Scrabble, if that's your taste.

8. MONDAY

A good day to start any new project. Don't keep your good ideas to yourself: friends or relations may be willing to help with special skills or money if they are put fully in the picture. Fill in an application form, it may be for a part-time activity or a study course, that has been hanging around for some time. Don't try to compete for attention with a charismatic Crab tonight, or you will come off second best.

9. TUESDAY

Follow your generous instincts today, and your life will become more fulfilling, spiritually and materially. You will be asked to play a more active role in an organization to which you belong. If you accept, you will have the chance to make friends with people you have long admired from a distance. Worry about a child or loved one will force you to confront a problem that you have been hoping to avoid.

10. WEDNESDAY

You will be invited to take a journey with friends, but the pressure of work at the moment will probably make this impossible. You'll certainly feel the need for a break, preferably in the company of someone special. Try to arrange a weekend away for the end of the month, when you should be less busy. You're in danger of getting your wires crossed tonight, when you could mistake a put-down for a come-on.

11. THURSDAY

Be careful who you confide in, for your revolutionary ideas may arouse fierce resistance. One of them you should put into action immediately: your ingenuity and audacity will win influential support. Later in the day you'll be taking physical exercise: it could be a sponsored walk for charity. Someone who has been hovering wistfully on the outskirts of your life will find the courage to make an approach this evening

12. FRIDAY

Your recent hard work has attracted attention. If you ask for a salary increase or promotion today, you will get what you want – although not immediately. Someone you meet around midday will become either a useful business associate or a romantic friend. Advice from a colleague will help solve a personal problem. If you've been waiting for the right time to make an important announcement at home, this is it.

13. SATURDAY

A chance meeting with someone from another country will leave you with a burning desire to take a holiday there, but be wary of trying to change holiday plans already finalized. If you do, you will certainly lose money – and may even end up with no place to go. Someone in your immediate social circle will now find that they are expecting a child. Could you be the Piscean who is now to become a mother or father?

14. SUNDAY

Many hands make light work on the home front, where team effort will bring success in a difficult job. If all the family muck in, you will save money on a repair that you thought would need professional attention. An elderly relative may try to help; be patient, although their efforts are in vain, they mean well. You'll be happy tonight if you pick up the telephone and re-establish contact with an old friend.

15. MONDAY

You will be feeling fed up with your job today, but rather than rushing off to look for a new one, seek to change the work system in which you now find yourself. Consult your workmates; they are as anxious as you are to see a certain restriction removed. Stand firm in a financial negotiation: if you're selling something, don't take less than you think it is worth. Exert yourself to cheer up a sad Sagittarian tonight.

16. TUESDAY

Seize on any opportunity that you are given to travel today. Someone you meet in a new environment will be able to give important advice that will further your career. Be security conscious, and take special care of all personal belongings: the indications are that you could mislay something of value. Love will stare you in the face at a social gathering tonight. You might at least say hello!

17. WEDNESDAY

Everything will run so smoothly at first that you will be in danger of becoming complacent. Keep your guard up: there is hidden danger from someone you have unwittingly offended. They are ready to seize on any indiscretion on your part in order to embarrass you. Cultural pursuits are favoured tonight, when you may make a new friend when attending a concert – or perhaps when changing your library book.

18. THURSDAY

Don't become discouraged and demoralized if business or personal associates seem narrow-minded and unadventurous. They are not yet ready to listen to your ideas; save them for early next week, when support will be easier to find. You will realize that an important change in domestic routine is necessary for your peace of mind. A partner may object, but your seductive wiles should put them in a more receptive mood.

19. FRIDAY

Someone will try to use financial pressure to get you in their clutches. Their methods amount to blackmail, so forget your Piscean reputation for saintliness, and fight dirty! You will not find it difficult to find evidence of their crooked behaviour in the past. Threaten them with exposure, and they will quickly back down. Romantic success tonight is problematical, especially if you're dating a Libran.

20. SATURDAY

A package you've been waiting for turns up this morning. Later, you will triumph in an unfamiliar field. If you have recently taken up a new sport or hobby, you will achieve something that only recently was beyond your wildest dreams. A medal or award for a special skill is indicated. Celebrate your success with friends tonight, and don't forget to say a special 'thank-you' to a partner for his or her belief in you.

21. SUNDAY

If you were hoping for a peaceful day, you'll be disappointed. Relatives, partners and family members are all down in the dumps, and seem to be expecting you to cheer them up. Their moaning will get on your nerves, and you'll be tempted to tell them to sort out their own problems – which are mostly of their own making. You'll have to make an effort though, otherwise they may go on complaining all week.

22. MONDAY

Take a positive attitude, and ignore the attempts of envious friends or colleagues to belittle a new project. If you stick to it, it will considerably increase your social or business status. Refuse an invitation that is extended to you at lunchtime; acceptance will involve you in unnecessary expenditure. If love really is never having to say you're sorry, you'll be spared a lot of explaining tonight!

23. TUESDAY

News delivered this morning by a colleague or friend will confuse you. Double-check that you've got the information right before taking any decision; then act as your intuition dictates. Ignore an unpleasant person who accosts you during a short journey this afternoon. Single Pisceans who are now looking for new accommodation will find that negotiations in connection with a flat will go smoothly.

24. WEDNESDAY

You've so much to do that your head will be in a whirl. Get your priorities in order, and deal only with essentials. If you dig your fingers into too many pies, you will fail to pull out a juicy plum! A new outfit worn today will be thought eccentric by some, but your partner will approve. If you've been cheating on a Scorpion lover, the cat will be out of the bag tonight – and you'll get badly scratched!

25. THURSDAY

Considerations of pride and prestige will lead you to think of ending a long-standing business or social relationship. If you do, you will later realize how much you depended upon it for security – but then it will be too late. Your judgement is not at its best now, so avoid all hasty actions. They say that you travel the fastest if you travel alone, but without loving support now, you will not travel at all.

26. FRIDAY

Remember the recent struggles you've had to make ends meet and don't allow colleagues or even family members to take financial advantage of you today. Refuse all requests for loans, whatever security may be offered. Stick to your principles, even if you have to hurt the feelings of those nearest to you. Live for the moment in a romantic encounter tonight – because that's all the time you are going to get!

27. SATURDAY

You should not try to take the initiative today. Your mind will be cluttered and confused, and events will be beyond your control. Sit back and let others make the decisions for a change. You'll have a pleasant afternoon if you fall in with a partner's plan for an outing to a new shopping centre or market. Don't go fishing in deep waters tonight: all you're likely to come up with is a cross-grained Crab.

28. SUNDAY

You are still feeling rather stressed, so you must try to take it easy. The colour yellow seems to be particularly associated with relaxation today. The behaviour of an animal belonging to a visiting relative will annoy you; perhaps another member of the family could get the creature out of the house? Something you read in a newspaper will provide you with the solution to a personal problem.

29. MONDAY

Energy returns, and you will summon up increased self-esteem to counter your recent bout of self-criticism. Communications will be difficult, with people liable to misinterpret your signals, but if you can work alone you will make good progress. You will be forced to accept responsibility for a mistake made by someone else. Keep things light in a social encounter, or the going will get heavier than you intended.

30. TUESDAY

Progress at work will be hampered by delays and complications that are beyond your control. Many trivial and irritating interruptions will distract you unless you put up a firm 'No Trespassing' sign. However, beware of failing to recognize a well-intentioned gesture by a colleague, or their feelings will be badly bruised. If your partner tends to put you up on a pedestal, you will fall off it tonight!

31. WEDNESDAY

The forecast for today is positive and progressive, when the fruitful exchange of creative ideas with both business and social contacts is indicated. You are suddenly offered a welcome change in your conditions of work. It may involve more travel: make sure that this would not unduly upset relations with a partner. You will think you hold all the aces in a contest with a lover – but they have trumps hidden up their sleeves.

JUNE

1. THURSDAY

You will be able to forget tension at home in a happy atmosphere at work and good relations with colleagues. You'll have an exciting appointment at lunchtime, but don't get so involved in a fascinating conversation that you miss an important meeting scheduled for the afternoon. Your persuasive powers are at a peak, which will come in very useful when you succeed in averting conflict with a neighbour this evening.

2. FRIDAY

Abandon your natural independence, and try in every way to co-operate with colleagues or family members. It's an excellent day for communications, so catch up with correspondence and make telephone calls that you have been putting off. Unattached Pisceans who have been admiring a new workmate from a distance will find that this is a good time to make an initial approach. If at first you don't succeed – forget it!

3. SATURDAY

A bright start to the day, with news of financial gain arriving in the post. You may permit yourself a modest bet: a horse with the name of a town or country should run well today. While you're waiting for the result, you'll get on with a much-needed repair job. You'll get more satisfaction out of intellectual activity with a partner tonight, even if it's only talking in bed, than from physical romps.

4. SUNDAY

Were you careful to put all your tools away after finishing that do-it-yourself job yesterday? Check now, for there is some indication of a minor accident to a child this morning. Don't be discouraged by a minor setback in a negotiation over property: you're on the verge of a breakthrough. The afternoon will find you in a garden – maybe basking in the sun, or more likely struggling with a lawnmower!

5. MONDAY

You will be aggressive in defending your beliefs this morning, when they come under attack by someone in authority. Speak your mind freely and you will win respect. Later, your work will take you out into the open air, and you will be able to combine business with pleasure. Resist an urge to go on a spending spree; later this week your partner will make demands on your pocket that cannot be ignored.

6. TUESDAY

Don't go looking for opportunities today – just stay long enough in the same place and they will come to you. If you go out on your travels, you are in danger of getting lost; and if people don't know where you are, you will miss the splendid offers they now have in store for you. Unless you keep a watch on your chattering tongue, you will have only yourself to blame for a ruined social occasion tonight.

7. WEDNESDAY

Before you attempt to put a plan into action, ask
yourself honestly if you are now being too ambitious.
Carefully weigh up your knowledge and skills. You
may well decide to aim at a more modest target.
Have no regrets: better a small success than a
shattering failure. You will be in mental sympathy
with your lover tonight, so take the opportunity to
have a serious talk. You'll find time for fun later.

8. THURSDAY

You will be amazed by an apparent personality
change in a loved one, and will wonder if you have
done anything to upset them. You have not – and
you must let them have the freedom they need to
seek for whatever it is they now desire. Sometimes
the best way to hold on is to let go. You will have to
give a friend a stern warning to stop their meddling
in your affairs. If this fails, a complete break must be
made.

9. FRIDAY

General resentment has been building up against a
workmate, and today you will be asked to join the
'lynch mob' that has formed. Either stay out of it
altogether, or take the side of the unpopular person,
who is not guilty of the offences charged. If you
support them, it will put you to much trouble in
return for small thanks, but you will have the
satisfaction of knowing you have acted like a true
Piscean.

10. SATURDAY

There will be a domestic row over an article of clothing borrowed without permission. You may be called upon to patch up both the row and the garment in question! Let hidden things stay that way. If you go prying into a partner's secrets, you will have only yourself to blame if what you discover hurts you more than them. You could be faced with having to end a valued relationship simply because your pride is hurt.

11. SUNDAY

You will realize with something of shock that in a few weeks' time you'll be off on holiday. The tickets and the accommodation are all in order – but what about you? Will other people at your resort think a Zeppelin has landed among them, or a whale has been stranded on the beach? This could be the day to start a diet – and don't pig out at a social occasion this evening.

12. MONDAY

Builders at work on or very near your home or workplace will cause you annoyance. There will long delays, noise, mess – and one colleague or member of the family may have an allergy triggered by dust or building materials. You will just have to make the best of it; it will end soon. You will find that a romantic contact has been pursuing you with an ulterior motive. Their hidden agenda concerns a third person.

13. TUESDAY

A great day for creative initiative. The success of plans made now may soon enable you to make changes in your life that you thought were impossible. Begin by fixing an appointment with a powerful person, who will welcome your invitation. Your social life is well starred, so don't turn down the chance of what seems likely to be a dull outing tonight. There's someone at the venue whom you really ought to meet.

14. WEDNESDAY

For business or social reasons, you will have to travel to a town you've never before visited. Your obligations will be quickly discharged, and you'll take the chance to explore. Don't stop to talk to an odd-looking stranger, or you'll have to fight off a pressing invitation to join a weird religious cult. You will be able to recover a sense of tranquillity if you visit a noted cathedral or art gallery.

15. THURSDAY

You will be feeling up-tight, and will need to fight off an inclination to worry about things that may never happen. Take life as it comes now: if you try to force things to happen, they will go off at half-cock. Repress the urge to snap off the head of a social contact when they annoy you, or you will miss out on an invitation to a prestigious event. A loved one will surprise you with a generous gift.

16. FRIDAY

You're the cock of the walk today, but beware rivals who will try to push you from your perch. The competition will be friendly, but in earnest – and it could harm you to lose status now, when important people are watching. You will be inclined to give encouragement to a new admirer who seems shy, but although it may be flamin' June, it would be wise to be flamin' careful – especially if an Arian is concerned.

17. SATURDAY

A dispute will arise with a partner or friend over travel plans. You are in the right, so make your position clear: things must be done your way or not at all. Otherwise a disaster threatens. Allow the dust to settle before you think of entering into another argument, this time concerning joint financial arrangements. You will need to give way on this issue and this will lead to peace at last – so breathe a sigh of relief.

18. SUNDAY

You will discover that an age difference in a romantic relationship is giving rise to malicious gossip in your social circle. You will oppose it, and will make it clear that you'll have nothing more to do with anyone who spreads it. Later, you and partner will find pleasure in a trip on or very near water. A family picnic is indicated. Get an early night, you're likely to be wakened very early tomorrow.

19. MONDAY

Take no nonsense from a colleague who tries to exploit your good nature. Other people will back you if you take a strong stand now. At home, it's a time for frivolity rather than serious effort. A gang of friends descends on you tonight, and what is on the cards appears to be a card party. Put on the green eye-shades, get out the liquor and potato crisps (prawn cocktail, if you must!), and shut up and deal!

20. TUESDAY

An exciting and rewarding day, when your abilities will impress people in positions of power. You will be offered the chance to take on new responsibilities, but at the cost of some freedom of movement. You will have to decide whether monetary reward will compensate for being more firmly tied to the workbase, with less chance to get out and about. A minor ailment may send you early to bed tonight.

21. WEDNESDAY

Your passion for change will annoy certain persons, who will claim that you are selfish and inconsiderate. Don't let them derail your train: the way forward today lies in competition, not co-operation. This is a good time to broaden your sphere of operations, for you will be able to gain the support of people who do not normally form part of your circle. A partner will need cheering up tonight.

22. THURSDAY

An emotional storm at home will leave you feeling drained. Comfort yourself with the thought that the cause of the quarrel was trivial and that it allowed you to get a few things off your chest. It will be forgotten by the end of the day. You won't make much progress at work: clear up simple but boring tasks that have been left unfinished. Solo Pisceans will let their hair down and go bare-headed for romantic fun!

23. FRIDAY

You will need to exercise all your sensitivity and diplomacy when an action you take at work is badly misunderstood by a superior. Don't panic when you are accused of dishonesty: explain matters clearly and simply and it will all end happily. A partner will object to your desire to go out alone this evening. Do not give way: your personal freedom is of vital importance to you, and rightly so.

24. SATURDAY

Any financial negotiations will prove difficult. On a shopping trip this morning, you will have a violent argument with a dishonest tradesman. Luckily, other customers will back you up. On no account sign, or even discuss, any legally-binding contracts or agreements. A relative's advice on your domestic budget will not be worth taking. Thank goodness for an understanding partner who knows what you need for relaxation tonight!

25. SUNDAY

It's time to do a little unseasonable spring-cleaning, both in the home, which is looking like a tip, and in your mind, where you are getting into a bad habit of self-doubt. Rope in all the family to deal with the first problem. The second you must tackle yourself, although loved ones will be anxious to give you reassurance if you ask for it. You'll end the day in a brighter mood than you began it.

26. MONDAY

Now that your emotions are back on an even keel, you'll want to make a voyage of adventure. You'll have the chance today to enjoy the company of unusual and exciting people. The experience may be more expensive than you would like, for you'll have to bear your share of the cost of lavish entertainment, but it will be worth it. A leopard cannot change its spots – but tonight you'll learn that a Lion can change its mind.

27. TUESDAY

The day begins and ends happily, but the hours in between will be a bit of a struggle. Good news comes in the post – but so does a large and unexpected bill. Differing opinions on a holiday for children will create tension between you and your partner. A relative you don't like will surprise you with their support in the row. Your opinion will prevail and your differences will be made up by bedtime.

28. WEDNESDAY

New responsibilities will confront you; you'll find them highly stimulating, although a bit daunting at first. Financially, you begin to feel secure at last. You will consider an extensive home improvement scheme, or even a move up-market, but make sure you weigh up the long-term financial implications. You will decide to break free from a restrictive association, but escape may be harder than you expect.

29. THURSDAY

You will be forced to act in a way that goes against your principles in order to counter a challenge to your career or social status. Take advantage of support from older authority figures who are friends of your family. Generosity towards one less fortunate than yourself will be rewarded in the long run. Your journey home will be unusually prolonged this evening, when a sudden bus or train strike is possible.

30. FRIDAY

An interesting development on the work front will hold out the promise of further improvement in your finances. Don't start celebrating yet: the outcome will not be certain until later in July. A heavy responsibility in connection with an elderly relative will be made easier to bear by the help and support of your nearest and dearest. An exciting book will give you a chance to escape from reality for a while.

JULY

1. SATURDAY

An argument over a long-standing domestic problem begins the day. It can be settled if a compromise is made over the household budget, with both you and your partner agreeing to accept economies in personal spending. The money you save will be earmarked for the purchase of a labour-saving device. You will get pleasure from creative and intellectual pursuits which involve other members of the family.

2. SUNDAY

A household task that you made a mess of yesterday can be successfully completed this morning. Family members will put you under pressure to make an expensive excursion, possibly to a theme park. Better give in, or they'll give you no peace. Fancy-free Pisceans will find that what happens tonight when they date another Fish will make the scales fall from their eyes! There are better fish in the sea, so keep trying!

3. MONDAY

The emphasis is on love and marriage. If you are single, you may begin a relationship with someone older, more successful and more serious-minded than yourself. If so, you should be aware that this will necessitate sweeping changes in your life-style, some of which you will not welcome. Pisceans with existing relationships will find that they take on greater permanence as a result of what happens today.

4. TUESDAY

If you commute to work, your arrival will be delayed this morning. Once you're there, people will seem a little strange, and are liable to act in uncharacteristic ways, but you will feel so healthy and confident that you will not care. Don't act on the basis of a rumour until you have thoroughly checked it out. In the emotional sphere, everything is securely tied up – but you may feel rather tied down!

5. WEDNESDAY

A domestic crisis will force an unwelcome change on you, and certain personal plans will have to be sacrificed. However, by the end of the day you'll decide that this may have been to your advantage. Waste not, want not: don't buy a supposed bargain you're offered around midday. Beware of flirtation: if you play Russian roulette with your emotions tonight, you are very likely to get your head blown off!

6. THURSDAY

The behaviour of associates will be unpredictable, so try to get on with your work alone. If you do not, you will get involved in a power struggle or battle of wills between two senior colleagues, and will be landed with the difficult task of peace-maker. Don't forget to buy a present for someone close to you who is approaching a birthday. You'll take a pleasant trip in the company of friends this evening.

7. FRIDAY

Your popularity at work will pay an unexpected dividend. The indications are that you will be asked to head a social committee, or organize a presentation. In any case, your status will be increased. A family member will oppose a certain career plan, but the person closest to you will be understanding and supportive. This evening's most beautiful moments will come about in a place far away from home.

8. SATURDAY

A well-starred day for any Pisceans beginning a holiday: the sun will shine on all your activities. Foreign parts also figure largely in events for stay-at-homes, who will receive exciting news from abroad. If you've planned a go-as-please holiday and have made no firm arrangements yet, it would be best to delay your departure. Otherwise you could miss an important development on the work front next week.

9. SUNDAY

Stay in your own goldfish bowl today, Piscean! Sharks are on the prowl outside, and if you go out to indulge in buying, selling or bargaining, you will get badly bitten. Single Pisceans should think twice if they get the urge to contact an old flame: it may be better to let sleeping Sagittarians lie. You'll be eager for second helpings after tasting the fruits of love with an inventive partner tonight.

10. MONDAY

You will start the day with an inspired business idea. It's as good as you think it is – but don't put it into action yet. Keep it secret until circumstances are absolutely right for its launch: next month will provide an excellent opportunity. Last-minute holiday arrangements can be safely left in the hands of a partner. A change of scene tonight will provide you with all the stimulation and recreation you desire.

11. TUESDAY

Communication difficulties – possibly a breakdown of transport, or a malfunctioning computer – will cause trouble, and may keep you away from work. Use the unexpected spare time to sort out some of your possessions: items from a long-abandoned collection may now be more valuable than you think. Later, a visitor you are expecting will be very late in arriving. Be wary of making any romantic commitment now.

12. WEDNESDAY

Politeness pays off for Pisceans today. Use your natural charm, and you will overcome another's lack of courtesy and avoid an angry confrontation. Take an opportunity to return a favour done by a friend last week, but keep over-generous instincts in check until you have assessed your financial position. A journey with one you love will give you the chance to discuss an important personal matter.

13. THURSDAY

Pisceans on holiday can expect an exhausting but rewarding day. Watch out for minor accidents if you're on the beach or in the sea: oily patches or floating jelly-fish could cause damage or annoyance. For those at home, it may be time to start taking a hobby more seriously: financial gain could result. Romance will be enjoyable, especially if you agree to undertake a joint project with a partner.

14. FRIDAY

When you count your money today, you will find you have more than you thought. It will be easy to solve a financial problem that occurs around midday. Something that happens at lunchtime will promise renewed happiness from a former romance, but you will decide that a present relationship is more important. Luck will be on your side this evening, so long as you act with discretion when dealing with a friend of a friend.

15. SATURDAY

You will get routine household jobs out of the way in record time, so that you can take a trip to a distant shopping centre. You will find the journey well worthwhile. Something you buy will make you decide to cut out some dead wood in your home: that rickety table may be on its way to the dump! You'll be the belle or beau of the ball tonight, although not everyone will admire your choice of partner.

16. SUNDAY

An older relative's advice on a financial matter will be worth hearing, but their scheme will need revising before it's put into practice. A lunchtime get-together will threaten to become rowdy, and you will need to exert a calming influence. Wave a gentle olive branch rather than a sledgehammer! Trust your intuition if you want to avoid a row this evening, when decisive action must be taken in a romantic tangle.

17. MONDAY

Don't let your ambitious drive tempt you into trying to manipulate workmates today. They will be in rebellious moods, and not at all inclined to follow your lead. In any case, a delay in your career progress now will be beneficial: it will give you the chance to hone a recently-acquired skill that you will soon need. Tonight, make full use of your temporary ability to see a partner or lover's hidden motives.

18. TUESDAY

What you think is a trivial idea may be more original and impressive than you realize. Try it out on a more experienced friend or colleague, and be guided by their reaction. Schedule an important meeting for late afternoon, when your powers of persuasion will be at their greatest. You will be wise to listen to a partner who will now warn you that an old habit of yours threatens to become a destructive force.

19. WEDNESDAY

You will be feeling dissatisfied, but if you count your lucky stars, you will find there are more than you thought. Impatience at work will lead you into a dispute, and if you insist on having your own way it will be the worse for you. Flexibility on your part is needed to bring out the best in others, as you will discover when you fall in with a partner's suggestion for an evening activity.

20. THURSDAY

If you can concentrate on the areas in which you are particularly talented, you will be in great demand today. However, don't take on too much: if you try to do too many things at once, you'll find you can't do any of them well. You'll learn something new around midday. Your energy and sex appeal will be overwhelming this evening, so be prepared to make allowances for a partner who finds it hard to keep up with you.

21. FRIDAY

Disappointment will rule your day. You will be expecting news from abroad, but it won't arrive. An anticipated change at work or in the home fails to take place. You will throw a tantrum, but no one will take any notice. Because of a partner's absence, you will have to untie a knotty domestic problem singlehanded. Solo Pisceans cannot expect any luck in romance tonight, when a favourite venue is closed down.

22. SATURDAY

A new acquaintance of a different nationality or colour from yourself will offer you the chance to take part in an unfamiliar activity. Go along with them: you'll have an enjoyable and fascinating experience. If you're leaving on holiday today, check your luggage labels: you'll get cold even in Zanzibar if your clothes are in Zagreb! Don't put emotional pressure on a partner; you still won't get your own way.

23. SUNDAY

It does no harm to believe in miracles, but you'll be making a bad mistake if you rely on one now. Only straight thinking and intense effort will get you out of a romantic mess in which you now find yourself. You've been two-timing a partner and have been found out. Now that you've lost them, you realize how much they really meant to you. Remember that with luck and persistence, lost things may be found again.

24. MONDAY

Peace and love will be mighty hard to come by today. The lurking shadows of financial concern and emotional insecurity lie across you, and you will look for support and find none. You feel like a sinking ship that even the rats have abandoned. Cheer up, things can only get better – and will, if you take the appropriate action. What that is, you may learn from the current 'problem page' in your favourite magazine.

25. TUESDAY

Make 'prudence in all things' your motto, and you will begin to climb out of the pit in which you have lately found yourself. Don't sit and mourn, but focus all your energies on recovery. A simple economy will cure your money worries. An honest confession will clear the air on the romantic front. When you need someone to lean on, partners or friends will be ready to stretch out a helping hand.

26. WEDNESDAY

The stars are ready to put a shine back in your life, but you must help them. Don't lie around waiting for opportunities to be offered – get out there and sell yourself! You have the gift of the gab today, and people will listen to you. If you've been unemployed, you should receive an interesting proposition now, but you must be willing to travel. Love may blossom in the open air tonight: follow your nose.

27. THURSDAY

Pisceans now on holiday will find this an unforgettable day. You will attend an exotic ceremony or view a spectacular sight. If you're at home, it's a time to think more of yourself and less of others. Don't let the stubbornness of a friend or partner stop you from improving your self-image in the way you think best. Young Pisceans may find themselves strongly attracted to an older person.

28. FRIDAY

Whether you're at home or away, travel will bring unexpected benefits. You'll make a contact that will prove to be of great importance to your social or business life. You will surprise your friends with a dramatic scheme for the redecoration of a room or house. At work, it's a good day to ask for a salary increase. Tonight you'll be looking for a one-to-one romance, but you may end up in a two-to-one mess.

29. SATURDAY

Don't exclude a distant relative from a family conference, for they could make a valuable contribution to a debate concerning a child's education. A trip with friends to a distant market place will turn out to be cheap and cheerful: you'll find nothing to buy, but you will enjoy window-shopping. If you need to discuss a delicate sexual matter with a partner, tonight will be a good time to do so.

30. SUNDAY

A younger member of the family will ask your advice on a tricky personal matter. Be very careful what you say and how you say it: any hesitation or sign of embarrassment is liable to be misinterpreted. Ask the help of an older person if necessary. Later, you will get in touch with an old friend you have been neglecting. Their news will distress you: they are in bad trouble and will need your assistance.

31. MONDAY

You have been under considerable stress recently, and it is time to relax and get into better shape both mentally and physically. Concentrate on your health and well-being today: it might be worth contacting a doctor for a full check-up. An exercise class or a new sport, possibly squash or badminton, could be the answer. Try a tisane (herbal tea) instead of your usual bedtime drink; it may help you sleep better.

AUGUST

1. TUESDAY

If you haven't already been on holiday, you'll be feeling the need for a break now. Routine tasks will seem harder than usual, and creative thought will be beyond you. However, don't neglect career matters altogether, for you are now attracting attention from those in authority. Keep up a bold front for the benefit of watchers. For the time being, your private life remains quiet and uneventful.

2. WEDNESDAY

What begins as a crisis turns out to be a blessing, when a personal disaster gains you the sympathy of a very important person. This is your chance to forge a relationship that could have a profound effect on your career and social life. There will be another exciting event later, but on an intellectual rather than emotional level. You may receive an award for a creative project you have recently completed.

3. THURSDAY

The changes now taking place in your career will impinge on your home life. A lengthy family discussion will result, when you will be called upon to state clearly where your real priorities lie. You must weigh financial security against emotional responsibilities. If you are planning to buy a new home or do extensive rebuilding, something that happens this afternoon will make funds easier to raise.

4. FRIDAY

A discussion with a superior at work will be misleading. You will assume that a decision has been made, but in fact the situation is still open to change. Go ahead only if you are absolutely certain of success. Your judgement in emotional matters is now so clouded that you should avoid important decisions. Soon, however, you will have to decide whether there is any future for an on-and-off romance.

5. SATURDAY

You'll get an intriguing offer in the post, and will be tempted to accept immediately. Ask around first: it may be above board, but accept the advice of friends if they say it's a scam. Two people with the same first name will compete for your attention later; the older one may have more to offer. Solo Pisceans who are dating a person in one of the caring professions will find that they too are beginning to care.

6. SUNDAY

It will pay to watch what you eat today, when some kind of tummy trouble is indicated if you are not careful. Social activity is well starred otherwise, particularly if you visit relatives you have not seen for a while. A child's misbehaviour may cause some damage, but it will be easily mended. It would be wise to show enthusiasm for a close friend's idea, even if it does not appeal to you.

7. MONDAY

You will be faced by an avalanche of paperwork. Tackle it methodically, for anything not completed by the end of the day will cause difficulty later. A colleague will give you a small gift: could this be a prelude to a romantic approach? An important piece of office or domestic equipment will go wrong. On no account should you try to fix it yourself, or you will do more damage. Call in professional help.

8. TUESDAY

This is an excellent time to seek for self-improvement. You will be given the chance to undertake a study course in connection with your work; the acquisition of a foreign language is indicated. Acceptance will make demands on your free time, but will much improve your career prospects. Something has to give if a romantic relationship is to survive, and you will be called upon to make the sacrifice.

9. WEDNESDAY

You will have to reveal another person's secret in order to clear yourself of a charge of cheating. It has to do with money, which will be the dominant theme of the day. If you are on holiday, you will be tempted to spend far more than you can afford on souvenirs. If you must buy, check that your treasures are genuine local crafts – not 'Made in Taiwan' (unless you happen to be in Taiwan, of course!).

10. THURSDAY

The stars smile down on communications of all kinds, and any suggestions you put forward now are likely to meet with approval. A pleasing career move will occur, but it will also make you realize that all advancement calls for some sacrifice or compromise. In this case, you may have to forfeit the company of a much-liked colleague. Solace yourself by spending a convivial evening in the company of old friends.

11. FRIDAY

You will feel frustrated because you cannot do things exactly as you wish. When others refuse their support, you will think you are neglected and unpopular. Snap out of it! It is only because you are over-reacting to trivial reverses that people are avoiding you. Be fun to be with, and they'll be with you. The only real disappointment you'll have comes in a financial negotiation with a partner this evening.

12. SATURDAY

Eccentric and self-willed behaviour will be your downfall. Your reckless attitude towards a current domestic problem will infuriate all the family, and make your home a scene of irritation and anger. You will have to make an effort to harmonize your values with those of your nearest and dearest if you are to reach an understanding. Pisceans swimming free may find that they raise Leonine libidos tonight.

13. SUNDAY

You will spend most of the day in the open air, whether it is at home or on holiday. In the latter case, you'll have to do some fast talking to end a holiday romance without leaving scars. Better choose a different venue next year! At home, the garden will claim your attention. Let someone else guide the mower for a change, while you score brownie points by volunteering to give a hand in an elderly neighbour's garden.

14. MONDAY

Commuters will have a nightmare journey this morning, but dejection will be swept away by welcome changes on the work front, where a change of scene – probably a move to a new office or building – is indicated. A misheard telephone message may cause confusion at a mid-afternoon meeting. You'll decide that physical chemistry in a relationship is not enough: you need someone who is also your intellectual match.

15. TUESDAY

Headstrong or rash behaviour will land you in a conflict with someone in authority. Take special care if you're driving; for then authority may wear a blue uniform! If you can control your rebellious tendencies, you can benefit from an individual approach to an influential person, who will welcome one of your ideas. A disagreement with neighbours may occur later; try to keep your temper!

16. WEDNESDAY

Your energy level is high, and your forthright approach to your work will evoke the admiration of colleagues. Shrug off a brief crisis of confidence that strikes when you are asked to undertake a confidential mission; you will succeed with the help of an unexpected ally. Your evening has an international flavour: you may be talking with students at a language school, or entertaining a guest from another country.

17. THURSDAY

Accept an offer made by an employer. You will be tempted to bargain, but they are unlikely to go any higher and may even withdraw it if you argue too fiercely. Later, be very careful if you find yourself sexually attracted to a person with whom you have business dealings. Let a partner have their say first in a domestic dispute: this will give you time to marshal your arguments so that you can demolish their case!

18. FRIDAY

If you own or operate a fax machine, an unpleasant message will upset you this morning. Show it to someone in authority, and ask them to take action. A friend you meet at lunchtime will give you good advice on personal relaxation, but you may find that the therapy they recommend is too expensive. If you care about 'politically correct' behaviour, you'll detest the person you date tonight.

19. SATURDAY

If you want company, you'll be disappointed if you sit around waiting for invitations to come through the door or for the telephone to ring. You'll have to take the initiative. Make a plan for a fun day; then call friends and ask them to join in. You'll get a good response, especially if your ideas for entertainment have an outdoor setting. Piscean saintliness won't stop you from raising the devil in romance tonight.

20. SUNDAY

Sporting pursuits are indicated for the earlier part of the day, when you may find yourself in the saddle. Don't neglect to wear any recommended protective clothing. Lunchtime will bring an interesting encounter with a person wearing dark glasses. If you feel restless, work in the garden this afternoon. Tire yourself out so that you'll want an early and undisturbed night: your partner is in no mood for romance.

21. MONDAY

Think positive, and don't underestimate your abilities. You feel that career or domestic responsibilities are fencing you in, and you long for space and freedom. If you put your mind to it, you will find a way to please yourself as well as others: ruthless reorganization of your present routine may do the trick. If a partner tries to stir up a bit of a row tonight, tell him or her you'd rather have a bit of the other!

22. TUESDAY

You will waste much of the morning in a useless dispute with a colleague over a trivial matter. Admit that you are in the wrong (even if you're not) if that is the only way to end it. You'll soon be good friends again. Careful checking of any mathematical calculations is essential. Unattached Pisceans will begin an unexpected affair. It will be a passionate diversion, and will not develop into a lasting relationship.

23. WEDNESDAY

Any career or financial uncertainties you experience today will prove to be unfounded. There will be a new and positive development concerning house or flat property. In the personal sphere, you will worry because a partner gives you little encouragement when you offer to help them. Are you sure that your attention to their needs has not grown so great that it threatens to become smothering?

24. THURSDAY

The intentions and motives of employers and colleagues will be a mystery to you. Don't try to solve it: any approach to them will be rudely repulsed. Work steadily on your own and you will make good progress. So good, in fact, that you'll be able to leave early. Pisceans who use the extra leisure time to look for love must beware: tonight could see you jump out of the sentimental frying-pan and into the romantic fire!

25. FRIDAY

An excellent day for travel, whether on business or pleasure, when you will be stimulated by meeting new people. Your journey will take you among people whose ethnic origin and culture is different from your own: learn all you can, for they have much to offer. Be adventurous when you are offered unfamiliar food; you will enjoy it. Generosity will be rewarded, whether it is strangers or friends who benefit from it.

26. SATURDAY

You will be feeling pleased with yourself if you have taken full advantage of recent opportunities. While in this mood of confidence, rearrange your domestic routine to suit you better. Take no notice if the family object; they will soon realize that the changes will benefit them too. Physical exercise in the open air is indicated this afternoon. Your understanding and tact will mend a damaged relationship.

27. SUNDAY

Your career is moving along nicely, your financial position is secure for the time being; so why do you feel vaguely dissatisfied? Perhaps you have only just realized that there is much more to life than material success. Pisceans have a 'psychic' sensibility: bring yours into play now to help in refining and reshaping your personal life, and in off-loading responsibilities that should no longer burden you.

28. MONDAY

Someone who has opposed you in the past will back down today. They will offer friendship, and will agree to your peace terms. You will be able to trust them from now on. Good timing will be of utmost importance to a midday meeting. Although your romantic activities now are quite open and on the level, you will take a secret pleasure in learning that gossip and rumours of scandal are going the rounds.

29. TUESDAY

Try to get any pressing work or appointments out of the way by midday, for you will need to make time for an important meeting this afternoon. It will concern your personal life, and may involve a former lover you had almost forgotten. Their sudden reappearance may cause embarrassment in a new relationship. Unattached Pisceans must go carefully too: it's time to take a breather in a whirlwind affair.

30. WEDNESDAY

Beware of making a martyr out of yourself today, when you will collect lame dogs in the way that some people collect stamps. Everyone wants your help: from a workmate struggling with a technical problem to an old friend with romantic troubles. Give advice by all means, by try not to get too involved. Haven't you got enough problems of your own, without volunteering to carry other people's baggage?

31. THURSDAY

Watch what you say today, when a sharp tongue will
cut both ways. What you see as a good joke at work
will be regarded by others as proof of your
irresponsibility. A careless remark to an
acquaintance at lunchtime could cost you an
invitation to a desirable party. You will think it
funny to describe a friend's painstaking paintings as
'just like Rolf Harris' – but they will not appreciate
your cruel wit.

SEPTEMBER

1. FRIDAY

Today marks a turning point in your affairs, with the first of a series of changes in both your work and social spheres. Things that are going on in secret now mean that very soon any stress and strain that has afflicted you recently will begin to seem like a bad dream. If you've been disillusioned and feel disinclined for further romantic entanglements, someone you meet tonight will make you think of changing your mind.

2. SATURDAY

Good news in the mail this morning, probably the announcement of a birth or wedding and an invitation to family celebrations. Partners and friends are sensitive to your needs, and you will feel happy and relaxed. Any excitement will come during a shopping trip, when you will find an ideal present for a loved one. Unattached Pisceans may suffer a broken date tonight – but they will find even better company.

3. SUNDAY

Although you will begin the day in a restless mood, stick to tried and trusted friends and pastimes, for experimentation is not well starred. The same applies to food: an exotic meal eaten today could have unfortunate consequences, with a disturbed night and bad dreams. Partners and friends will not seem eager for your company tonight, but perhaps it is because they are planning a pleasant surprise for you.

4. MONDAY

The wheel of fortune is spinning fast, so get your
stake down at once if you want to make a profit.
You will feel apprehensive about approaching a
superior, but if you summon up your courage and
take a chance, a career issue can be resolved in a
way that exceeds your highest hopes. If you're
unattached, don't take on a 'difficult' lover in the
hope of reforming them. You will fail, and be hurt in
the process.

5. TUESDAY

All kinds of financial arrangements and agreements
must be handled with extreme care today. A parting
of the ways will occur in a business or social
relationship. If money is concerned, there will be a
dispute. You may have to consider taking legal
action to protect your interests. It will also be
necessary to reappraise a domestic partnership,
where responsibilities need to be put on a more
equal footing.

6. WEDNESDAY

You will experience a burst of energy, but make sure
that it is properly harnessed and directed. Otherwise
you will simply waste the day in disputes over trivial
issues. An acquaintance will approach you with a
business plan, but you must refuse to speculate or
invest if your instincts warn you to be cautious. You
will spend the evening leading a family discussion
over a major move.

7. THURSDAY

Something that happens in a public place this morning will teach you a difficult but useful lesson. Later, you will have to compromise or back down in a business dispute; continued resistance could endanger an important project. A partner will annoy by asking you to take over their domestic tasks tonight. You should agree: they have a problem that you know nothing about as yet, and need time to sort it out.

8. FRIDAY

Make a careful note of any unusual events in the business or domestic spheres today, for they will provide pointers towards changes you must shortly expect. Don't issue an ultimatum when someone opposes a plan: try to find an alternative instead. You could win an argument – but that doesn't necessarily mean you are in the right. Solo Pisceans may find their rose of romance blighted by a scornful Sagittarian tonight.

9. SATURDAY

Solitude will not appeal to you, but neither will over-exuberant company. Seek out an old friend with whom you can enjoy a quiet and restful day. You will both enjoy a visit to a country market town. Take a word of warning: if you give way to the physical attraction you begin to feel for your companion, trouble may result. Don't change your plans tonight in order to satisfy another's wishes.

10. SUNDAY

Some domestic problem, probably in connection with the fabric of your home, is indicated. Have you checked the roof for loose tiles lately? A person you meet around lunchtime will offer help with a business scheme, but you will be in two minds about their trustworthiness. Give them the benefit of the doubt for the time being, but watch them carefully. Don't let pride damage your relationship with a loved one.

11. MONDAY

Be content to pursue your ambitions slowly and methodically. Over-enthusiasm and hasty actions will only lead to delay and disappointment. A new friend will prove intellectually stimulating, and may inspire you to take up voluntary work for a worthy cause. Make sure that this will not demand time and attention that you should give to family matters. You will be able to finalize a domestic rearrangement tonight.

12. TUESDAY

Self-employed Pisceans will have had a nasty financial fright recently, but what happens today will give you a new sénse of security. The set-back was only temporary, and there are good times ahead. Be sure to turn up for a lunchtime meeting with friends, where you will hear more good news. If you try to sweep a romantic problem under the carpet, it will come creeping out to embarrass you when you least expect it, so face up to it.

13. WEDNESDAY

You will find it necessary to ring the changes in the company you keep. A certain friend has made one demand too many on your emotions or pocket, and it is now time to give them their marching orders. Stand firm at work when an older colleague tries to sabotage plans. At home there will be changes for the better, but unless you speak frankly to a lover, a sexual hang-up will continue to bother you.

14. THURSDAY

Elderly or housebound Pisceans can expect a welcome visitor, who will come with a gift. If you're at work, you will need to insist on fair play when someone else claims credit for a task you accomplished. Don't be afraid to make a fuss. A reunion with an old friend will occur around midday. If you decide to take them out on the town tonight, make sure you have plenty of cash in hand, for they will have expensive tastes.

15. FRIDAY

Any work connected with publicity, promotions or advertising is especially well starred. A partner or lover will make a surprising appearance at your workplace. Do not be alarmed: you will welcome the news that they have brought you. You will be tempted to back down from a confrontation with an aggressive person at a social occasion tonight – but stand your ground and they will give way first.

16. SATURDAY

You will be tempted to blame a child for an article or sum of money that has gone missing. Restrain yourself: the lost property will turn up later in an unexpected place – where you put it! A relation you haven't seen for some time will remind you of an old ambition, and will show you how to accomplish it. A partner will throw a wobbly over a trivial fault: you will think they're acting childishly – but don't say so.

17. SUNDAY

If a certain relationship is to survive, it is now essential that you spend some time without seeing the other person concerned. You need a breathing space in order to sort out your true feelings. Take a solitary walk or drive in the country; or throw yourself into some strenuous sport if your talents go that way. Solo Pisceans be warned: you are expecting too much from a lover who wants to keep the romance light.

18. MONDAY

Sweetness and light prevail at work this morning, when you will find colleagues eager to help you. The afternoon brings a challenge from a workmate of the opposite sex that will endanger one of your career goals. It will be hard to judge what your options are:

try to leave things open until tomorrow. Your home life is under luckier stars, and any conflict that has arisen recently will be ironed out tonight.

19. TUESDAY

An in-depth conversation that lets you know exactly where you stand will enable you to take a more laid-back attitude to a work relationship. The tide turns in a financial matter, and you will be able to make an ambitious and long-desired purchase – probably an electrical appliance. You will decide that something is missing from a passionate relationship. You know what it is, but you are reluctant to face the facts.

20. WEDNESDAY

A powerful but hidden influence is working in your favour, so try not to be discouraged by today's delays and frustrations. Regard any progress you make, however small, as a bonus to sweeten a taxing time. A legal problem that has preyed on your mind will be solved without the expense of professional advice. Romance is in the air tonight, but you may be too tired to spread your wings in pursuit.

21. THURSDAY

If you sincerely want to get rich, something that happens today will swell your coffers. It's a great time for doing deals of any kind, but don't keep your mind completely wrapped up in your money-bags, or you'll miss a chance for success on the social front that is offered later. If you recently split up with a romantic partner, a combination of circumstances this evening will throw you together again.

22. FRIDAY

A good day for seeing farther into a mill-stone: your intuition verges on the psychic ability with which Pisceans are said to be specially gifted. People's motives are an open book to you, and many things of which you were unaware will now be revealed. You will know instantly how best to take advantage of them. One hunch you'll act on is to invite a stranger into your home, and this will prove an excellent move.

23. SATURDAY

Your home will seem cramped; to avoid becoming tetchy, get out and about. An outing with younger relatives or children will prove rewarding, but keep a close eye on them if you find yourselves in a high place. Intellectual stimulus will be needed later. Try a movie of the kind you wouldn't normally watch, and it might help you see your own life from a different angle. Don't let money problems sour a romantic relationship.

24. SUNDAY

Greed will cause a problem if you let yourself be tempted into either physical or emotional over-indulgence. Too much to eat or drink at a lunchtime celebration could result in a wasted and miserable

afternoon – and possibly a social calamity too.
Throwing a fit as a result of a partner's trivial
mistake could embitter your relations for days.
Practise self-restraint and you will avoid these
pitfalls.

25. MONDAY

A colleague whom you have underrated will make a
time-saving suggestion that it will pay you to adopt.
Make sure they get the credit for it; don't try to
claim it for yourself or you will be found out. Be
wary of the friendly advances of a stranger you meet
at lunchtime: if you invite them into your life, their
part in it may be a sinister one. Keep your defences
up tonight, when an Arian makes a determined
assault.

26. TUESDAY

You will be wise to spend as much of the time as you
can in quiet contemplation. Your energy is low, so
go into action only when it becomes absolutely
necessary. Exercise compassion this afternoon when
someone approaches you with a hard-luck story: not
all down-and-outs chose to be that way. At home,
don't let an obsession with a plan of your own blind
you to the merits of a partner's suggestions.

27. WEDNESDAY

Although it will not be easy for you to
compartmentalize your life, you must do so now. If
you allow your emotional problems to intrude on

your work space you will do yourself harm. Tell a partner or lover that they must moderate their demands on your time and patience. Single Pisceans looking for a mate tonight will find that unconventional dress and behaviour is the best bait.

28. THURSDAY

Seize upon any opportunity to travel today, when new contacts will prove particularly advantageous. Draw up a timetable before you start out and stick to it, or you will miss a certain appointment and be forced to make an annoying back-track. A friend's recommendation will be of great help with a business contact. Later, the well-being of a partner will be the deciding factor in a problem that you must solve.

29. FRIDAY

Time spent in instructing a new and inexperienced workmate will not be wasted; you will gain a useful ally in a forthcoming power struggle. If you grant a favour that is asked, relations with a partner will be harmonious and intellectually stimulating. You'll be riding on the crest of a wave at a get-together tonight, but then a crafty Capricorn will try to put the skids under your surf-board.

30. SATURDAY

Lose no time in getting on with a constructive project – not necessarily involving bricks and mortar – at home. Only persistence will guarantee success. You will have to deal with a friend who is stirring up trouble for a mutual acquaintance. Their intention is good, but their information is dead wrong. A missed telephone call will bother you all evening, but don't fret – it wasn't who you thought it was!

OCTOBER

1. SUNDAY

A child's minor accident or illness will throw your plans for the day into confusion. An outing with relatives will have to be cancelled. This will make you feel penned in, and you and your partner will plan a weekend break for yourselves in the near future. You will have to make economies in your personal spending to be able to afford it. Ask relatives if they will agree to look after children or pets.

2. MONDAY

A tendency to bossiness is the only thing that could bring failure on a day when everything should go your way. Don't try to order colleagues around, or there will be trouble. Lead from behind, and use your subtlest wiles to make them believe that what they are doing is their own idea – not yours. Make sure that any disagreement with a partner is ironed out before bedtime, or you will have a restless night.

3. TUESDAY

Partnerships of all kinds will go out of control today unless you act with strength and determination. You will need to be adamant in demanding that others honour their obligations and promises. Don't extend the hand of friendship – they'll try to bite it off. Wield the whip instead! An expensive gift from a lover cannot necessarily be taken as proof that they are not cheating, or that they never intend to.

4. WEDNESDAY

An association with someone abroad will be ended
today by a letter or phone call. Do not grieve: the
relationship had run its course. What you must do is
settle all outstanding bills while you still have the
money in hand. If you put things off any longer, you
will have serious trouble later this month. A partner
will show a lack of sympathy – perhaps because they're
tired of your harping on one particular problem.

5. THURSDAY

An anonymous love letter that comes this morning
will give you a thrill, but be wary, for it may be a hoax.
Some crafty questioning of a friend known to fancy
this kind of trick is called for. In a work problem,
you'll get help from a younger colleague and will see
light at the end of the tunnel – and it's not an
oncoming train! Now you can begin to think of
making a move that you have been planning for some
time.

6. FRIDAY

Don't insist on having your own way in a
reorganization of facilities at work. If you do, you'll get
what you want – and then kick yourself because your
obstinacy has cost the chance of getting something
better. Listen carefully to the instructions of a superior,
or you will make a bad mistake. You've provided a
shoulder to cry on often enough: now a lover must
face up to the fact that their troubles are of their own
making.

7. SATURDAY

A friend will suggest that you try a course of acupuncture to relieve a minor health problem: it is certainly worth consideration. Harmony rules at home, where loved ones are understanding and supportive. You will get pleasure from the cultural achievement of a young relative or child; be lavish in your praise. Solo Pisceans will find that tender talk will pave the way for tactile tactics tonight.

8. SUNDAY

Murphy's Law rules, OK? That's the one that says that anything that can go wrong, will go wrong. Machines of every kind seem to be ganging up on you. The car won't start; the spin-drier won't spin (or dry); the dishwasher chews up the best china and spits it out in little pieces. You would like to give Mr. Murphy a piece of your mind – but since you can't, don't take it out on your nearest and dearest!

9. MONDAY

If you bite off more than you can chew, you'll end up eating humble pie. You will need the support of others in anything you undertake. If you scorn their help and try to go it alone, you will make a mess of all your tasks. Don't accept an offer of overtime or a 'moonlight' job, or you'll risk total exhaustion. Confidence in your ability to cope is a fine thing, but this is a time to be more laid back.

10. TUESDAY

Dynamic self-sufficiency will make you feel like a big fish in a small pond, and you'll certainly make some waves. Colleagues or partners will be content to follow in your wake, while you have a whale of a time. Today will see a great surge upward in your career or social status. You could well see your name in print this evening, when a letter or article you have written may appear in a local newspaper.

11. WEDNESDAY

Try to be sympathetic when a colleague or friend comes to you with a personal problem. It's one you've heard before, and it's all their own fault – but they are more desperate than they seem, and badly need reassurance. You got through so much work yesterday that you now have increased leisure time. You will feel like loud music, but don't inflict it on your neighbours! There are good sounds at a new club nearby.

12. THURSDAY

Live now, pay later, is your motto. Try at least to get routine tasks out of the way before you abandon yourself to pleasure. Blown to the shops by a biting wind, you'll splurge on a new top-coat, scarves, gloves and winter woollies. You may be broke later, but at least you won't be cold! You'll entertain friends tonight, and will be stunned by a declaration of affection from a most unlikely quarter.

13. FRIDAY

The stars will send little tests to tempt and challenge you. Provided you don't upset an important person with a petulant display of bad temper, you will get through this day of ill omen without damage. In fact, you could attract additional funds into your bank balance if you accept a chance that's offered this afternoon. Discretion will prove a virtue tonight, when hungry Lions will be on the prowl.

14. SATURDAY

Good news for all Pisceans with a large and hungry family to cater for: this is a great day for finding bargains in foodstuffs, possibly at a discount warehouse. It will be cheapest to buy in bulk: so make a list of staple necessities, compare prices carefully, and then pile the trolleys high. It's a good day for selling too: if you are disposing of a car, you'll get a good offer this afternoon.

15. SUNDAY

Head for the countryside this morning, when all the family will welcome a trip to catch autumn leaves. (For every leaf you catch as it falls, they say, you'll have a happy day next year.) You'll plan a quiet evening, but a horde of uninvited guests will pile in. It's a good thing you bought so much food yesterday! Young and fancy-free Pisceans are warned that too much ardour tonight could frighten away a shy Scorpion.

16. MONDAY

However reluctant you feel to face up to things, you'd better take your head out of the sand or problems will creep up and kick you in the rear! If you don't make certain changes of your own free will, worse solutions will be forced on you. Colleagues and partners will be unpredictable and offer little help. You'll have to relax your grip on the romantic past before you can begin to plan for the future of a new relationship.

17. TUESDAY

Social ambitions climb high today, and you will be in no mood to be ignored. Don't shout too loudly, or you'll deafen the ears you want to reach. Watch out, too, for the plotting of a jealous acquaintance. Someone you meet around lunchtime could further your ends: you will recognize them by a yellow garment. You will be worried when certain events reveal just how much power you have over a romantic partner.

18. WEDNESDAY

When you have to take a back seat today, remind yourself that it's not as bad as having to push the car. The triumph of a colleague attracts everyone's admiring attention, and if you can't offer sincere congratulations, you'd better keep silent. Things improve later, when you'll remember that when the gorse is not in bloom, kissing's out of season. Remember also that gorse flowers all the year round!

19. THURSDAY

No matter what disruptions and upheavals are threatened at home, you must now struggle as hard as you can on the work front. This is the ideal moment to bring off a great coup you have planned for some time: miss the chance now, and it's gone for ever. If a partner accuses you of neglect, explain just what is at stake, and make them see that they will have a rewarding share in your career success.

20. FRIDAY

Travel, possibly to an unexpectedly long distance, is indicated for today. It will be a busy and complex journey; at times your head will reel because of the amount of information you are required to take on board. You will be intense in expressing your views, and will probably have some fierce arguments, but all your contacts save one will be fruitful. The dud one you'll recognize by a familiar smell!

21. SATURDAY

Family members will drive you half crazy with demands for a revolution in domestic arrangements, while you are quite satisfied with the house as it is. Pretend to agree, and persuade them to start by shifting the heaviest furniture. They will soon get tired and give up! You'll eat a take-away meal, but beware of over-indulgence in an exotic pickle. Single Pisceans could meet a soul mate at a soul gig.

22. SUNDAY

The early Fish catches the worm! If you give up your Sunday lie-in, you could be in time to grab a real bargain at a nearby car boot sale. It may be an item you or a partner needs to fill out a collection. Don't let your elation make you careless on the way home: some risk of a road accident is indicated. Get all members of the family together this evening for a serious discussion on the domestic budget.

23. MONDAY

Not for the first time this year, your emotional life intrudes into your work environment. You must settle this problem here and now – and without creating a spectacle in front of inquisitive colleagues. It will be wisest to request time off, but a superior's remark may make you feel that the ground is not as steady under your feet as you thought it was. Spend the evening alone, cooling off and making plans.

24. TUESDAY

Just because you have experienced reverses lately, don't assume that you are doomed to failure for the rest of the year. Patience and hard work will win respect and will put your career back on course; despair will get you nowhere. All will be well so long as you leave nothing to chance. Do not delegate even the simplest, most routine jobs to other people, or you will be held responsible for their mistakes.

25. WEDNESDAY

A chance remark will lead you to examine personal
habits that may be holding you back in business or
social life. They may be mental failings. Do you fear
failure too much? Do you feel that people don't like
you? These can be cured by positive thinking. On
physical habits, ask the advice of a close friend. They
have been longing to warn you about an annoying
mannerism, but were far too polite to raise the
matter.

26. THURSDAY

A straightforward and relaxing day will come as a
relief after recent upheavals. Your diplomatic skills
have returned, and all around you are persuaded to be
friendly and supportive. Someone will surprise you
with warm thanks for an act of kindness you had
almost forgotten. Later, tough talking will do nothing
to forward a sticky romantic relationship, but sweet
nothings could lead to something good.

27. FRIDAY

A colleague or friend will let you down in the worst
possible way. Don't throw a wobbly, or all the
sympathy will go to the guilty party. Instead, draw out
the traitor with honeyed words, until all can see how
badly they have behaved. You will also need to keep
your emotions under control when a partner confesses
that they have misused a joint savings account. Don't
rage; try to find out why they did it.

28. SATURDAY

Someone who has decided that you are a soft touch will be made to realize how mistaken they are, when you rise up in passionate anger to protect a member of your family. This could be a crunch day for single Pisceans: a proposal (either by you or to you) for a permanent partnership or marriage is indicated. You will have to think very seriously: it may be best to delay either your question or answer for a few days.

29. SUNDAY

If a person close to you takes you for granted, it will be your own fault. You are trying too hard to conform to the picture they have of you. Today you will lose nothing, and may gain much, if you show them your true self. You have an important question to ask a friend, but do not take a chance that presents itself around midday or you will not gain the favour you seek. Temper your passion with practicality tonight.

30. MONDAY

Your world of work will seem especially humdrum, and you will long for adventure and new experiences. Resist the urge to kick over the traces: discipline and organization today will be well rewarded. If you feel that you are in a rut, break out in other ways. Join a club that will provide a new leisure interest, whether it is sky-diving or crown green bowling. Take up needlepoint embroidery – or take a new lover!

31. TUESDAY

An unavoidable monthly expense will be added to
your domestic budget. The economic mini-crisis it
causes will make it necessary to boost your income.
Family members who have been unco-operative of
late will now rally round, and one will offer to take
a part-time job to help out. This evening, get to
grips with a tricky task you've been putting off: you
now have the discipline to make a success of it.

NOVEMBER

1. WEDNESDAY

A disagreement early this morning will leave you feeling unsettled, and your judgement will be poor. Double-check all paperwork, especially if it concerns money, and avoid getting into any arguments. Someone you often see at lunchtime is becoming a drain on your time and pocket; you will now seek to end the relationship. Hurry home tonight: a loved one is out of sorts and needs your attention.

2. THURSDAY

Business or social obligations will force you to make a long journey. There is some indication that a domestic crisis may arise in your absence. Make sure your partner knows where you are going, and if circumstances delay your return journey, be sure to call them. Don't get involved in the problems of a stranger you will meet by chance. Solo Pisceans will find everything's coming up roses in romance, and it's time to pick a few!

3. FRIDAY

What happens this morning will mark a turning point in your working life. Whether it is for the better or the worse will depend on what use you have made of recent opportunities. If you're disappointed, take heart from the fact that the situation can be retrieved by hard work in the weeks to come. Even if you've had a career set-back, there will be an improvement in your financial situation now.

4. SATURDAY

You will share equally in a partner's joy when good news comes by the morning post. On the minus side, you will feel that a cold is coming on: an 'old wives' cure' may prove more effective than an expensive patent medicine. Cultural activity is indicated this afternoon, when you may visit an art gallery or attend a concert. Have an early night in order to put paid to that cold.

5. SUNDAY

Even if you're feeling under the weather this morning, an invitation to spend part of the day with friends will buck you up. You'll have lunch out in a picturesque venue, but the food will be disappointing and will cost more than you intended to spend. Take the advice of a friend concerning an article of dress. Later you'll face a romantic temptation when you encounter an intriguing person dressed in bright colours.

6. MONDAY

An important person will have their eye on you, so work responsibilities will require your full attention. Even so, don't take things too seriously or tension will cause you to make mistakes. Have confidence, relax, and you'll take problems in your stride. Later, you may experience a minor breakdown when driving. Plumb the depths of passion tonight, and you will succeed in shifting an emotional blockage.

7. TUESDAY

You will be full of drive and energy now, but those around you may be off-colour, for a 'flu 'bug' invades your workplace. Do not be impatient with colleagues who can't keep up with you; you may need their sympathy before very long. If you do more than your share, it will be noticed where it matters. The promise of a new romance will turn out to involve more lager-and-lime than champagne cocktails.

8. WEDNESDAY

Partners and workmates will be going through a touchy phase, so avoid any suggestions that could lead to disagreement. An unexpected development around lunchtime should be welcomed, for it will enhance your social status. You will make it clear to a business associate that unless they make good on a promise, there must be a parting of the ways. Later, the words of a child will offer guidance and inspiration.

9 THURSDAY

A mission of mercy on behalf of an elderly relative will make you late for work this morning. Once there, you will be asked to take over the job of a senior colleague who is absent. This will boost your promotion prospects, but will involve you in working extra time for the next few days. This evening you should include a partner in an activity you normally do alone; this will greatly reinforce your relationship.

10. FRIDAY

Don't let the black mood of a relative or partner bring you down, for you will need all your enthusiasm to tackle a complicated work problem. You'll only have time for a brief reunion with an old friend around midday. When your task is successfully completed, you'll reward yourself with a long-desired treat. Romance will seem like a game of tag tonight, when you're 'it' and have to do the chasing!

11. SATURDAY

Nothing will go according to plan today, so just resolve to lie back and enjoy what happens – whatever it is. Perhaps your stars cannot pierce the fog that shrouds your neighbourhood now! There are vague indications that you will make a rewarding shopping trip. Relatives may visit in the afternoon. A piece of domestic machinery may go wrong. Normal service will be resumed as soon as possible!

12. SUNDAY

All the coughs and colds that are going about will remind you of the importance of a sensible diet and regular exercise. It's no weather for jogging, but you and a partner can enjoy gentle aerobics indoors. If you flop in an armchair all day, you'll have backache tomorrow! You will need to listen carefully to a young relative's questions about sex if you are to provide the reassurance they need.

13. MONDAY

News of an unexpected financial windfall will lead
to a family discussion. A partner says the money
should be spent on a memorable Christmas
celebration; you will favour putting it aside for a
dream holiday next year. If you've a large family, put
it to the vote of all members. If not, you'll have to
compromise. An encounter with a Virgoan of the
same sex as yourself will lift your spirits tonight.

14. TUESDAY

You will need to be flexible if you are to remain
open to new opportunities. It is, however, a bad
time to make firm commitments or finalize any
arrangements. Money will present a problem in a
loving relationship: you will need to come to a new
understanding over how it is to be divided and
spent. If you've been flying high in a new romance,
your wings will be clipped by something that
happens tonight.

15. WEDNESDAY

A colleague's offer will give you the chance to
escape from a burdensome work obligation. Make
sure you know what kind of favour will be expected
in return. In a personal relationship, be careful not
to let your desire for financial security overrule your
need for emotional equilibrium. You and a friend or
partner will take great pleasure in planning to take a
trip together in the near future.

16. THURSDAY

Maybe you're a good friend for anyone to have, but you're certainly a bad enemy. You prove this now, when someone who has insulted you or acted against your interests will be shocked by the violence of your reaction. You won't actually come to blows, but it'll be touch and go. You'll savour life to the full tonight, when you'll have the chance to launch out on an unfamiliar kind of adventure.

17. FRIDAY

Strange fears and imaginary worries will plague you unless you get your head in order. You'll need to look into your unconscious self to discover the source of these fantasies. When you have, you'll find it easy to reason them out of existence. Fantasy of a different kind rules tonight, when you will feel that you're living in a romantic novel. You'll need to do some rewriting if it's to have a happy ending.

18. SATURDAY

Activity is going on all around you, but while others are busy and contented, you will feel dissatisfied. You'll find it difficult to settle to anything, and the noise made by a repair man in the house won't help. Nor will a puzzling message that comes in the post. You will only be able to relax by yourself, and outside the home. Visit a quiet place: you could find peace of mind in an old church or lonely woodland.

19. SUNDAY

The day begins well, when you reach agreement
with a partner over a domestic responsibility that
neither of you is keen on accepting. A remark
overheard at a lunchtime venue will give you an
idea for an unusual holiday activity next year. If you
are honest with your lover tonight, an intimate
problem can be solved and something that has been
lacking from a sexual relationship will be found.

20. MONDAY

You will feel confused. You have done all the right
things in your determined attempts to get ahead, but
they seem to lead nowhere. You must put up with
this brief period of stagnation: what is happening
behind the scenes will soon lead to a time of great
creativity and constructive achievement. At least
you're getting somewhere in an important personal
relationship, which will take a further stride now.

21. TUESDAY

It's time for fine-tuning in your work programme.
Take a close look at the way you have organized
your routine. What may seem to be minor
adjustments to your schedules will, if you make
them now, have significant long-term consequences.
The odds will be stacked in your favour in a dispute
around midday. Losing a battle with a partner
tonight will make you a wiser and more experienced
opponent in future.

22. WEDNESDAY

People you mix with today will fall into two groups: those who cause trouble, and those who clear up the mess. Which one will you join? You will have to choose this morning, when an almighty row centring on an illicit romance (not yours!) will divide your workplace or social group. If you decide to become a peacemaker, your efforts will win admiration from both sides for your wisdom and maturity.

23. THURSDAY

Although you tend to resent being told what do, you will be wise to accept guidance from an older colleague or friend now, especially in financial matters. However, you will be able to assert your independence when you adapt and improve another's idea for the benefit of both of you. Watch out for a fast-talking stranger later. Efficiency and compassion will both be needed to heal a partner's wounds tonight.

24. FRIDAY

Many distractions will be offered, but you must concentrate on your work. You are in danger of making a mistake that will involve you in much delay next week. Since your finances are looking good and your fashion sense is at its keenest, this will be a good day to go shopping for clothes. Don't linger too long in the shops though, or you will miss a telephoned invitation to a celebration with friends tonight.

25. SATURDAY

Rather than waste time in arguing, you will accept the blame for an oversight that was really a partner's fault. You'll need to make haste if you are to be on time for a close relative's great occasion. The indications are that it's a christening or even a wedding party. Young and unattached Pisceans will be playing games tonight – and 'One-hunnn-dreddd-and-eighteeee!' will be the score when Cupid throws his darts.

26. SUNDAY

Gremlins must be infesting your home, for mechanical devices of all kinds will be on the blink. There will almost certainly be a row about who last used the screwdriver, and where they put it! The only way to deal with these malicious goblins is to ignore them: then they'll get bored and go away. So leave the house empty while all the family enjoys a drive in the country followed by a meal in an ethnic restaurant.

27. MONDAY

All you need today is one good idea. Don't be tempted to act on any half-baked notions or wild theories: get your mind in gear, come up with the ultimate solution, and you'll be on the way to success. This will improve your self-image: people who admire your talents would be surprised to know how little you think of yourself at times. Take a look in the mirror tonight, and you will like what you see!

28. TUESDAY

Chickens that emerge from eggs laid today will soon come home to roost, so be prepared to take the consequences of any dirty deeds you do now. You will have a chance to double-cross a colleague for financial gain. You will find a valuable piece of property that should be returned to its owner. An old flame will offer visions of a one-night stand. Beware, all these temptations have very nasty strings attached!

29. WEDNESDAY

A strange and vivid dream just before you wake this morning will spark off your creative imagination. If you work in the fields of fashion or design, this will be a red-letter day on which you'll make a lasting mark. Like other Pisceans, you will also come to realize that professional and financial success are not the be-all and end-all of life, and you will feel a hunger for deeper spiritual understanding.

30. THURSDAY

You will be in the mood to take charge today, but unfortunately the people nearest to you will strongly object to being pushed around. It will be better to take a back seat, for you can expect to profit from

the mistakes others will make without your
guidance. Tonight you'll feel like pulling the plug on
a romantic relationship – but are you really sure that
you want to see it go down the drain?

DECEMBER

1. FRIDAY

A difficult balancing act will be needed today. In order to convince others of the viability of your pet project, you will have to keep your feet on the ground while letting your imagination soar. Tonight you will visit a place absolutely new to you. There you will fall in love, but not necessarily with another person. It may be with an ideal cause, a revolutionary set of beliefs, or a whole new life-style.

2. SATURDAY

Light exercises will make a good start to a day on which you will need to be nimble. Like you, everyone else has decided to shop early for Christmas, and you'll have to weave your way through milling crowds. A sadder task faces you later, when you'll have to comfort a relative who has suffered a sad loss. You won't feel like making merry this evening, but board games with the family could cheer you up.

3. SUNDAY

Not for the first time, the sloppy habits of certain members of your family will drive you to distraction. However, experience has taught you that there's little to be done about them, so expend your energy more constructively. A visit to an art show or craft fair will provide you with some useful ideas for Christmas gifts. Draw up 'present' and 'card' lists tonight, or you're sure to forget someone important to you.

4. MONDAY

Let other people into your mind today. If you take the trouble to share your innermost thoughts with a romantic or business partner, they will give you the reassurance you now need. Don't rush to take responsibility for another's action, even though you may be partly responsible for it, or they will come to rely too much on your support in the future. A jealous Gemini will try to queer your pitch at a party tonight.

5. TUESDAY

Trust your own judgement when colleagues oppose you over a work problem. In order to get your own way, you will have to call in a favour you did for one of your opponents some time ago. In a romantic partnership, you will be the one faced with a demand to pay up, and you will have to give way over a major issue. You'll have a new experience this evening, but the stars are reluctant to reveal if it's a pleasant one!

6. WEDNESDAY

Pressure from friends and partners will be kindly meant. They think that you need shifting out of a rut – but you are quite content with the position you find yourself in now. Their support, however, will encourage you to take a chance on a business venture. It will not pay off yet. There will be so much chaos at home tonight that you'll be able to slip away to a secret rendezvous without anyone noticing.

7. THURSDAY

A workmate will be implicated in an unpleasant scandal, possibly involving a sum of money. Don't take sides in the matter, or you'll be on a two-way loser. A lunchtime outing will need to be cut short when a friend feels unwell. Someone will try to bully you into doing them a favour this afternoon: tell them to get lost! It's a good evening for some pre-Christmas hospitality, so invite congenial neighbours round.

8. FRIDAY

You will need to take the day off from work to deal with an urgent personal matter. It may concern the sudden illness of a near relative. Your superiors, whom your efficiency has impressed lately, will be helpful. Your mercy mission will be successful, and you'll relax with your nearest and dearest tonight. For solo Pisceans, tonight will see either the beginning or the end of a torrid affair with a bouncy Bull.

9. SATURDAY

A chance to put your relationship with a loving partner on a firmer basis will be offered, but a mental block from the past will prevent you from making the right moves. Only deep thought followed by plain speaking will remove the obstacle. You'll do better in a new association, where you'll make an influential friend. Follow the example of a younger relation tonight if you want to enjoy yourself.

10. SUNDAY

The only troubles you'll have today are within your own mind. Don't worry too much about the future, and don't let inner problems make you belittle your solid achievements. The colour green, or perhaps a person whose surname is Green(e), seem to be especially favourable to you. You must now take the initiative in a newly-begun romantic relationship, or a certain person will conclude that you are not interested.

11. MONDAY

You will forge ahead on the work front today, although a minor blip, in connection with a mistake in a letter, is indicated. Don't look for solo success: team-work will now bring better results. Something you buy at lunchtime will have a most beneficial effect on your appearance – and don't let an envious colleague convince you otherwise. Use stealthy tactics in romance if you want your grand strategy to succeed.

12. TUESDAY

Travel is indicated today. It may be that you will take a physical journey, or you may move a considerable distance in connection with a business negotiation. In either case, you'll make a false start, but end up satisfied with your progress. There will be a tearful scene at home tonight: you may have to comfort a child who has suffered a great disappointment. You'll be closely watched at a social function later.

13. WEDNESDAY

Any secret activities or negotiations in which you are involved must be handled with extreme care. There is a spy about: you may be able to recognize them by an expensive raincoat. If you yourself do a little spying, you will discover the solution to a long-term mystery. Stay close to your telephone (or switch on the answering machine) if you are self-employed, for an intriguing offer is on the way.

14. THURSDAY

The work atmosphere is relaxed, so you will devote most of the day to personal affairs. You will break a promise to a colleague in order to meet with a loved one at lunchtime. You'll eat in a special place that reminds you of your earliest encounters. Later, you will wish to make an angry protest about an injustice that has been done to a friend. Hold your horses: you don't know all the facts yet.

15. FRIDAY

Unorthodox behaviour will succeed best today, so when you find yourself in a jam, don't rely on familiar tactics to get out of it. Do the unusual and you'll fox the opposition. You're on a financial see-saw at the moment: weigh it down in your favour by deciding against the purchase of an expensive gift. If your social life is to broaden out, you will have to decide to abandon a certain belief – or a certain person.

16. SATURDAY

It's a good thing that a disturbance in the street wakes you early, for you have much to do. Get out those Christmas lists and shop till you drop! Crowds surround you, but everyone is in a good humour, and you will not have difficulty in finding what you need. You'll relax at home this afternoon – and pretend not to hear the doorbell. Loving partnerships will be a bed of roses tonight, with no sign of a thorn.

17. SUNDAY

You're all fingers and thumbs when it comes to doing anything practical today, so let someone else wrestle with the ribbons and sticky tape if you're wrapping parcels. A visiting relative will offer to cook the evening meal. Accept with thanks, but hide the best china – you're not the only clumsy one! Unattached Pisceans will find that mixed feelings about a new romantic partner will have them in a spin.

18. MONDAY

It will be difficult for you to trust anyone today. Remarks passed at work will leave you wondering whether your colleagues are trying to be honest, helpful – or just plain rude. It will be best to have as little as you can to do with people who may be feeling under the weather. An anonymous telephone call may upset you or a partner this evening. Put it out of your minds; you needn't worry about such rubbish.

19. TUESDAY

Power struggles and emotional battles will flavour the day. In the business sphere, you'll be working behind the scenes to undermine the self-confidence of a rival. On the personal side, you'll trip up a partner who imagines that they are firmly in control of your relationship. If you're unattached, you'll be resentful of a potential lover who is content to sit back and lets you make all the running in a new affair.

20. WEDNESDAY

The Christmas truce has begun, and all relationships are likely to be harmonious. The festive holiday hasn't arrived yet, so work problems will demand most of your time. Don't let social temptations prevent you from completing routine tasks, or you may have to miss a promising party on Friday. In spite of a slight financial worry, you'll decide to purchase an expensive present for a loved one.

21. THURSDAY

Past efforts at work will be rewarded in the shape of a generous gift or bonus. You will be involved in an argument at a shop where you try to exchange a recent purchase. You'd like to refuse an invitation to a function from a boring colleague, but if you don't go it will create bad feeling that will last into the New Year. Reports of a major political upheaval will make you have doubts about next year's holiday venue.

22. FRIDAY

Unless you're employed in one of the caring professions, when it will be a busy time, you will spend more time celebrating than working. Take it easy at lunchtime, or you could have a nasty fall. You'll feel like splashing money around: a camcorder may tempt you, in order to record the family Christmas. Evening will find you bustin' out all over at a social occasion – kindly adjust your dress before leaving!

23. SATURDAY

Whatever last night was like, it wasn't silent – or holy! Your sleep was disturbed by late revellers, and you will feel grouchy this morning. A meeting with friends around midday will cheer you up. Don't let your sense of humour get the better of you when visiting an elderly relative later: your idea of a joke will not be theirs. Romance is brilliantly starred for young and single Pisceans tonight.

24. SUNDAY

Resist the urge to rush out and make extravagant last-minute purchases: you already have all you need for a splendid celebration. This afternoon you will take a long walk with children: if you haven't any of your own, relations would be happy to have theirs taken off their hands for a while! You can brighten up a lonely neighbour's Christmas by inviting them to your home for a few hours this evening.

25. MONDAY

Merry Christmas! Be careful not to make it too merry in one sense, or you may have a disaster with the Christmas dinner! The unwrapping of presents will be interrupted by a long and welcome telephone call from a friend living far away. A relative who calls this afternoon will make a surprising announcement. If you're in love, you'll find satisfaction in sharing your mind, as well as your body, with a lover tonight.

26. TUESDAY

It wouldn't be Christmas without a crisis – and yours blows up this morning! A vital piece of domestic equipment goes wrong, and you can't fix it. Thank goodness a practical neighbour is able to make a temporary repair. You'll have to make a duty visit to dull relatives in the afternoon, but an unexpected guest who also arrives will liven things up. Unattached Pisceans will find it best to hunt in couples now.

27. WEDNESDAY

A social occasion of which you had high hopes will prove disappointing. You may meet a useful business contact, but the person you'll really wanted to see will be absent. Pisceans with families will have trouble with children who are feeling a sense of anti-climax. If you're sensible, you'll have booked seats for a children's show this afternoon. Later you'll relax and rediscover togetherness with a loved one.

28. THURSDAY

You may be back at work, but not much will get done there. When you've caught up on gossip, you will concentrate on clearing the decks in preparation for a big effort next week. You'll plan an evening at home, but a surprise invitation will see you celebrating once more. If you need a book at bedtime (but indications are that you'll have other interests), one on dieting would be a good idea!

29. FRIDAY

If you didn't suffer a hangover at any time during the holiday, you'll have one today – a financial one! Of course you've spent too much, but you had a good time, didn't you? You'll lock away your credit cards and plan rigid economies for the next few weeks. Unfortunately, you'll see an irresistible bargain at the next 'Sale' notice you encounter! Don't say yes to an eager Archer who will turn out to be a 'no-no'.

30. SATURDAY

Money still does most of the talking, when a joint financial arrangement with a partner gives cause for concern. You will plan to consult an accountant early in the New Year. You, or someone close to you, will be accident-prone, so make sure your first-aid drill is up-to-date and that you know where the band-aids are. What you think is a sexy outfit will attract more guffaws than gasps at a social function tonight.

31. SUNDAY

Unless you take it easy on the social front today, you will not be able to hear the bells that ring the New Year in. This will be even more of a pity if you are currently single, for you will miss the chance to begin a rewarding long-term relationship tonight. So stay awake and alert, and welcome in a year that holds great promise for all Pisceans. Maybe 1996 will prove to be the Year of the Fish.